The Prodigal Son

Discovering the Fullness of Life in the Love of the Father

Matt Carter

LifeWay Press®
Nashville, Tennessee

Editorial Team

Reid Patton
Writer

Susan Hill
Production Editor

Jon Rodda
Art Director

Joel Polk
Editorial Team Leader

Brian Daniel
Manager, Short-Term Discipleship

Michael Kelley
Director, Discipleship and Groups Ministry

Ben Mandrell
President, LifeWay Christian Resources

Published by LifeWay Press® • © 2019 Matt Carter

ISBN 978-1-4300-5529-7 Item 006104395

Dewey decimal classification: 226.8
Subject headings: BIBLE—PARABLES / PRODIGAL SON (PARABLES) / CHRISTIAN LIFE)

To order additional copies of this resource, write to LifeWay Resources Customer Service; One LifeWay Plaza; Nashville, TN 37234; fax 615-251-5933; call toll free 800-458-2772; order online at LifeWay.com; or email orderentry@lifeway.com.

Printed in the United States of America

Groups Ministry Publishing • LifeWay Resources • One LifeWay Plaza • Nashville, TN 37234

Contents

About the Author

MATT CARTER serves as the pastor of Preaching and Vision at the Austin Stone Community Church in Austin, Texas, which has grown from a core team of fifteen to over 8,000 attending each Sunday, since he planted it in 2002. Matt has co-authored multiple books including a commentary on the Gospel of John in *The Christ Centered Exposition Commentary* series. Matt also co-authored a novel of historical fiction, *Steal Away Home,* which tells the real life story of famed pastor Charles Spurgeon's unlikely friendship with former slave-turned-missionary, Thomas Johnson. Matt holds an M.Div. from Southwestern Seminary and a Doctorate in Expositional Preaching from Southeastern Seminary. He and his wife Jennifer have been married for over twenty years, and they have three children: John Daniel, Annie, and Samuel.

Introduction

Being a Christian is hard. There, I said it.

Wait a minute Matt, Jesus said my burden is easy and my yoke is light. And you know what? That's true. When I'm fully submitted to Jesus and walking well with Him, that verse makes all the sense in the world. My problem is that I have a pretty good track record of not consistently walking well with Jesus. Not because of Him, but because of me. Maybe that's not you're story, but it's mine. Christianity is hard. Worth it, but hard.

As a pastor for over twenty years, I've been preaching the Bible for a long time— been reading it for even longer. And when it comes to my biblical heroes, the ones that I have found over the years that I love the most, I love not because of the good they've done but, because of how they've failed. Why? Because I can relate.

There's a guy in the Bible, I definitely wouldn't call him my hero, or really a hero at all, but I can certainly relate to him. People often refer to him as "the prodigal son." If you grew up in church you know the story, but if you didn't here's the short version. This young man asks his dad for his inheritance before the old man dies. His father grants his wish and the young man takes off to a foreign land, then squanders his inheritance and is forced to come home with his hat in his hand. That's actually not how the story ends, but I don't want to get too far ahead of myself.

When I was younger, I couldn't relate to this guy. But now, years later, unfortunately, I can relate to the guy more than I ever thought possible.

If you're a Christian that has it all figured out, this book is not for you. If you're a Christian that's never really failed, fallen, or struggled– there might be a better use of your time than reading these pages. But, if like me, you love the Lord, but at times throughout your life you find yourself weary and broken, bruised and battered–maybe even hanging on by a thread—then this book is for you. No matter how weary you are, or how far you've fallen, your Father's love for you is greater than your wildest imagination. I wrote this book partly as therapy for myself, and partly as a guide for people like you. And hopefully, it will guide you back into the arms of a loving Dad ready to welcome you home, wipe you clean, and call you His beloved son or daughter.

Matt

How to Use This Study

This Bible-study book includes eight weeks of content for group and personal study.

Group Sessions

Regardless of what day of the week your group meets, each session of content begins with the group session. Each group session uses the following format to facilitate simple yet meaningful interaction among group members and with the truths of God's Word presented in this study.

START. This page includes questions to get the conversation started and to introduce the video teaching.

WATCH. This page provides space to take notes on the video teaching.

DISCUSS. This page includes questions and statements that guide the group to respond to the Matt Carter's video teaching and to explore relevant Bible passages.

Personal Study

PERSONAL STUDY. Each session provides two personal Bible studies. Each personal study works through the Scriptures to deepen their understanding of the week's topic. Each study includes questions and teaching designed to help participants understand the Bible and apply its teaching to their lives.

BIBLE READING PLAN. Additionally, each week of personal study provides four guided Bible readings that allow you to read related passages from the Scripture and learn to study them on your own. Each reading follows the REAP method, outlined on the next page.

The REAP Method

Each session features four Bible reading exercises, using the REAP method.

Read

Read the passages for today's Bible reading. Read the passages with an open heart, asking the Holy Spirit to give you words of encouragement, direction, and correction (2 Timothy 3:16). Underline the verses that stand out to you.

Examine

Spend some time reflecting and writing about what you've read. Write down one or two of the key verses that stand out as particularly important. Ask yourself these questions and write down your thoughts:

- What is going on in the passage?
- Who is writing and who is he writing to?
- When was the author writing?
- What are the circumstances that the author is addressing?
- Does the writer mention anything that might indicate his purpose or intent?
- How do you think the author wants his audience to respond?

Apply

After examining the passage, apply the text to your own life. Ask yourself these questions:

- What is God's word for me from this passage?
- How will I live differently and be different today because of what I read?
- What are the things in my life that need to change in light of this truth?

Pray

Pray through the passage and your application, asking God to change your heart and to change your life, based on the time you've spent in God's Word.

Week 1
The Problem

Start

Welcome to Session 1. Use these questions to get the conversation started.

Jesus frequently used parables to teach His followers what it means to know and follow Him. Over the next eight weeks we're going to go line by line through a well-known story known as the parable of the prodigal son.

Name one of your favorite stories.

What do you like about this particular story? What have you learned from it?

Stories engage our imagination in a way that other kinds of teaching doesn't. They guide us to see truths that we might not otherwise notice by allowing us to live vicariously through the characters in the narrative. The parable of the prodigal son offers the same opportunity. Whether this story is familiar to you, or you are hearing it for the first time, there's much we can learn from Jesus' teaching. As we study this parable together, we'll identify and answer some big questions that many of us have asked before or may even be asking right now.

Ask someone to read Luke 15:11-24.

Pray and ask God to use our time together.
After praying, watch the video teaching.

Watch

Use this section to take notes as you watch video session 1.

Video sessions available at lifeway.com/ProdigalSon
or with a subscription to smallgroup.com

Discuss

After viewing the video, discuss the following questions with your group.

Have you or anyone you know attempted to find a better life outside the love of the heavenly Father? What are some reasons we go and search out a "better life"?

Why are we hesitant to embrace the cost of following Jesus? What do we feel as though we are missing out on if we fully commit to Jesus?

Read Matthew 13:44. Why is the reward of following Jesus worth embracing the cost?

Following Jesus is always costly, but the reward outweighs the cost. When people encounter the life-giving, soul-changing, love of Jesus, they turn their backs on the allures of the world and they go all-in.

What changes when we begin to see Jesus as our greatest treasure worth losing everything else to pursue?

What do we miss when we see Jesus as merely a part of our lives instead of our whole life?

Reading a story like the prodigal son, it may be tempting to think, "I would never do that." But at some point, we all doubt the love of our Father. The temptation for the far country exists for all of us. If it doesn't right now, it will in the future. This story helps us see that no matter how far we roam, the best life is found in the love of the Father.

Where do you see yourself in this parable? Why should the parable cultivate sympathy for people who have wandered away from faith in Jesus or never experienced it to begin with?

Close your discussion with prayer. Remind those in your group to complete the personal studies and Bible reading over the next week.

Personal Study 1

Why Do People Walk Away?

The problem that lies at the heart of this study is the reality that an increasing number of people are coming to the conclusion that life is more fulfilling outside of God's love. But why is that? What keeps people from committing to follow Jesus? Interestingly, Jesus answered this question with another parable we find earlier in the book of Luke. This parable demonstrates several reasons people walk away from faith

Read Luke 8:4-15.

In this parable, seeds are sown on four types of soil. What are the four types of soil and what do they represent?

Jesus used parables to reveal important truths to His followers. Though this story is often called "the parable of the sower," the focus is not really on the sower, but on the soil in which the seeds are distributed. Each type of soil received the Word of God, and each soil responded differently. Looking at each soil helps us identify reasons people walk away from faith.

No Faith in the First Place

What kept the seed that fell on the hard ground from taking root?

Why should we have sympathy and compassion towards the people represented here?

Some walk away from faith without ever knowing or having faith in the first place. The initial batch of seeds fell on the hard dirt along the path, and the birds snatched the seed away before it could take root. This soil represents the people we know who reject God. The devil has blinded them from seeing the goodness of God (see 2 Cor. 4:4).

Who do you know in this situation? Pause for a moment and pray for them.

A Christian Home Isn't Enough

Just last year, a study from The University of Texas at Austin, reported that the number of college students identifying as Christians has dropped to only 2 percent. Alarmingly, statistics are similar across the country. One of the primary factors leading to this rapid decline is that kids growing up in Christian homes are going away to college and then walking away from the faith.

What happens when we assume that just because someone shows up at church or participates in religious activities that they're committed to Jesus?

Simply growing up in a Christian home doesn't ensure that faith is being passed on to the next generation. A Christian home is important, but it's not enough. Attending youth camp or worship events doesn't guarantee a child's faith is their own. Without a personal saving faith, they are like the seed on the rocky soil; there is an appearance of growth, but it can't be sustained because they never personally experience the life-changing salvation of Christ When mom and dad are gone, they walk away from the faith.

If you have children, in what ways are you intentionally nurturing and encouraging their growth?

Allure of the World and Shame of Failure

The third soil that Jesus mentioned is filled with thorns that grow and choke faith, "with worries and riches and pleasures of this life" (v. 14). The allure of the world was stronger than their faith in Jesus, so they pursued worldly temptations instead of Him.

> **The third soil is filled with thorns. In your experience, what are the "thorns" that make people chase experiences and comforts of the world instead of Jesus?**

> **When do you feel this temptation yourself?**

Another reason for the decline in Christianity is the increasing number of people of all generations who simply come to the conclusion that following Christ means missing out on the best life has to offer. With the third soil Jesus could also be describing those people who allow worry from past or current sins to keep them Jesus.

Most folks in this category grew up in church, so they know what God expects of them. So when a pattern of sin enters into their lives, especially a pattern of sin that keeps reoccurring—the weight of that guilt and shame causes them to just give up altogether and walk away.

> **How do unconfessed sins become barriers between us and Jesus that choke our faith?**

Lack of Committed Christians

How did Jesus describe the fourth soil?

The fourth soil that Jesus described was the one where the Word of God was received with joy and it began to produce fruit.

Unfortunately, true examples of committed Christians, those who embrace the Word of God and find their life in Jesus, are becoming rare. Far too many Christians have merely made Jesus a part of their lives instead of their whole life. Instead, some view Jesus as a friend who you reach out to when you need something. This shadow of true Christianity is neither compelling nor attractive. When young Christians see the older generation chasing material blessing while giving lip service to Jesus, what possible conclusion can they come to?

Who do you know who has fully embraced what it means to follow Jesus? What do you learn from their faith?

The fourth soil, the committed Christian, produced an abundance of fruit. Maybe you don't know a fully committed Christian, but that doesn't mean you can't become one. The Bible screams from the rooftops that the greatest and fullest experience of happiness and blessing is found in only one place, and that is in a full hearted, both-feet planted, total life commitment to the person of Jesus.

End your time today praying that God would help you commit to Him fully.

Personal Study 2

The Solution

So far in this study we've seen that many people are asking serious questions about what it means to follow Jesus. People all around us are asking, "If I follow Christ, what will it cost me? If I fully commit to Jesus, am I missing out on life's best?" What is the answer to these questions?

The answer is a resounding "no." In fact, the shocking answer is that the only life worth having is found in knowing God the Father through His Son Jesus Christ. This is the central claim of Christianity.

However, we need to realize that these questions are not new. People have been asking them since the first century. Jesus encouraged His disciples to ask. Today we're going to looking into one such account in the Gospel of John.

A Bold Claim

Read John 6:53-58.

Jesus did not literally mean that people should eat His flesh or drink His blood. What did He mean?

Why did the crowd find this statement offensive?

At this point in Jesus' ministry, huge crowds of people followed Him wherever He went because He was working miracles, feeding the hungry, and healing the sick. Jesus paused, looked at the crowd, and exclaimed unless the crowd ate His flesh and drank His blood they could not follow Him (v. 53). Jesus did not mean this literally.

By "flesh and blood" Jesus was referring to His whole being. In other words, Jesus was saying that unless they devoted themselves entirely to Him they could not find life.

Why is the claim that Jesus made still shocking?

How does this claim still offend people today?

The claim that Jesus made—that true and abundant life can only be found in Him alone, is the most shocking and inflammatory claim in all the world. And Jesus made this claim repeatedly. It offended people in the first century and it offends people today.

The swelling crowd following Jesus–drawn in by His teaching and miracles– didn't understand what He meant, so they turned and walked away. His disciples were standing with their mouths wide open, stunned that the popularity of their leader had just plunged—but Jesus was unmoved by it.

A Bold Response

Peter realized life is found in only one place—Jesus.

Read John 6:66-69.

What does Peter's confession in verse 68 affirm to us about Jesus?

What have you experienced while walking with Jesus that let's you know that Peter's confession is true? How have you found full and abundant life in Jesus?

All people are hardwired to pursue a life filled with purpose and meaning because we were all created to relate to God. Two-thousand years ago, Jesus made a bold claim when He said that the fullness of life can only be found in following Him, and following Him completely. The problem is that if we are not finding life in Jesus, we are looking for life in places we could never hope to find it.

Peter asked Jesus a straight forward question: "Lord, to whom shall we go?" Think for a moment about your friends who don't know God. Where do they turn to find life?

As you've watched these friends search for life in other places, what were the results?

We live in a culture where people are desperate for a different way to live. No amount of friends, success, accomplishments, money, promotions, or social media followers can give us the life we all so desperately desire. These things may make us feel good for a moment, but they can't ultimately satisfy us.

Those of us who know Jesus, have a responsibility to show other people the way to experience abundant life (John 10:10). How will the people around us see or know a better way if those of use who know Jesus aren't willing to show them? How are we going to turn the tide of death and despair riddling our culture if Christians live no differently?

How does the way you live show people what it means to follow Jesus?

This world desperately needs to be shown a new way. The world needs ordinary people, who decide to go all-in when it comes to following Christ. Our culture is desperate for a generation of believers that don't just make Jesus a part of their lives, but passionately put Him first and show this world with their everyday lives, that yes, there is a better path—a path of peace, love, and happiness.

What might you need to let go of to follow Jesus more closely? Is there anything you need to give up?

Think again about your friends, neighbors, family members, or maybe even other Christians, who are trying to find life by chasing the things of this world. What might it look like to have a conversation with them and point them towards Jesus?

End you time together praying that God will help you to find life in Jesus alone. Use Psalm 16:11 as a guide for your prayer.

You will make known to me the path of life;
In Your presence is fullness of joy;
In Your right hand there are pleasures forever.
PSALM 16:11

REAP
Luke 15:11-24

Further familiarize yourself with the story we will be diving into over these next eight weeks together.

Read   Read the passage slowly and carefully with an open heart, asking the Holy Spirit to give you words of encouragement, direction, and correction.

Examine   Pick a few verses and look at them more closely to gain a deeper understanding of what the Bible is saying.

Apply   Consider how you will live differently in light of what you read.

Pray   Pray through the passage and your application, asking God to change your heart and to change your life, based on the time you've spent in God's Word.

REAP
Matthew 13:44-46

Jesus told a series of brief parables to explain the true value of the kingdom of heaven. Nothing in life can give us what Christ's kingdom offers.

Read   Read the passage slowly and carefully with an open heart, asking the Holy Spirit to give you words of encouragement, direction, and correction.

Examine   Pick a few verses and look at them more closely to gain a deeper understanding of what the Bible is saying.

Apply   Consider how you will live differently in light of what you read.

Pray   Pray through the passage and your application, asking God to change your heart and to change your life, based on the time you've spent in God's Word.

REAP
Psalm 16:1-11

True and lasting pleasure is only found in the presence of God.

Read   Read the passage slowly and carefully with an open heart, asking the Holy Spirit to give you words of encouragement, direction, and correction.

Examine   Pick a few verses and look at them more closely to gain a deeper understanding of what the Bible is saying.

Apply   Consider how you will live differently in light of what you read.

Pray   Pray through the passage and your application, asking God to change your heart and to change your life, based on the time you've spent in God's Word.

REAP
Hebrews 3:12-19

The author of Hebrews provides a sobering warning about the deceitfulness of sin and its ability to lead to false beliefs.

Read   Read the passage slowly and carefully with an open heart, asking the Holy Spirit to give you words of encouragement, direction, and correction.

Examine   Pick a few verses and look at them more closely to gain a deeper understanding of what the Bible is saying.

Apply   Consider how you will live differently in light of what you read.

Pray   Pray through the passage and your application, asking God to change your heart and to change your life, based on the time you've spent in God's Word.

Week 2
The Lie

Start

Welcome to Session 2. Use these questions to get the conversation started.

In week 1 of the personal study we addressed several reasons people wander away from the Father. Which one have you seen most often?

Last week we looked at the central question in the story of the prodigal son.

Are we missing out on life's best by following Christ?

Surveying the world around us, it's undeniable that scores of people have answered, "yes" the best life is found by pursuing my own path. Rejecting God and pursing our own path is the essence of what the Bible calls sin.

But if we, as followers of Jesus, know sin never delivers on what it promises, we have to consider what leads people to sin in the first place. The Bible has the answer.

One of the amazing things about Scripture is although it was written two-thousand years ago, its truths are timeless and the Bible remains 100 percent accurate in diagnosing modern-day questions and problems. God knew His children would face a world where they would question whether or not following Him was the best choice. This week we will focus on the lie that led the prodigal (and us) to wander from home.

Share a time when you someone lied to you.

Ask someone to read Luke 15:11-12.

Pray and ask God to use our time together.
After praying, watch the video teaching.

Watch

Use this section to take notes as you watch video session 2.

Video sessions available at lifeway.com/ProdigalSon
or with a subscription to smallgroup.com

Discuss

After viewing the video, discuss the following questions with your group.

What's shocking about the request the younger son made to his father? What must he have believed about his father to make such a request?

How do our beliefs influence our actions? When have you ever made a poor decision based on an incorrect belief?

The younger son's request was bold and cruel. He was essentially saying, "Dad, I wish you were dead. I'd rather have your money than you." For him to make this request, the son had to believe life in the far country was better than life in his father's house. Similarly, when we pursue sin, it's because we have believed the lie that disobeying God will be good for us. In this week's teaching, Matt said there were two primary reasons we believe lies: our sinful nature and the devil.

If we know sin is wrong, why does our sin always seem like a good idea at the time? How does our sinful nature affect our choices?

Read John 8:44. How is the devil described in this verse? Why is it helpful to know who the devil is and how he operates?

Observing the world around us, what lies are the people around you most prone to believe?

What are some ways we can help people see beyond the lies and to redirect their focus to the life that is only available through faith in Jesus Christ?

Close your discussion with prayer. Remind those in your group to complete the personal studies and Bible reading over the next week.

Personal Study 1

The Origin of the Lie

For the last decade, our culture has been obsessed with superhero movies. At the publication date of this study, the Marvel Cinematic Universe features three "phases" comprised of twenty-three separate movies, with another phase and five more slated to release over the next two years. We can't get enough of these stories. And like all good stories, these movies all have great beginnings.

You may have noticed many of these movies begin the same way. You're introduced to a hero. He or she charges on the screen and dispatches a threat to let you know who they are and what kind of powers they have. Next you're shown, usually by way of a flashback, the hero's origin story. This narrative element gives the audience some sense of where the character came from—maybe they were exposed to gamma radiation or perhaps they were bit by a radioactive spider.

All of humanity has a common origin story revealed to us in the opening pages of Scripture. This origin story explains who we are and how our world came to be the way that it is. The Bible tells us a story of God, a man, a woman, and a garden. Everything was perfect until a serpent crept into the story and told a lie the man and woman believed, and the world fell into sin and darkness. The Bible shows us where sin came from and how to overcome it.

We're going to tackle those two ideas in this study and the next. First, by taking a closer look at sin's origin story, then in the next study we will see how to overcome its influence. Since this all began with a lie from the devil, let's take a closer look at him.

In this week's video teaching we heard from Jesus concerning the devil:

> *He was a murderer from the beginning, and does not stand in the truth because there is no truth in him. Whenever he speaks a lie, he speaks from his own nature, for he is a liar and the father of lies.*
>
> JOHN 8:44

How is Jesus' description of Satan different from the cartoon version our culture asks us to believe?

What are the dangers if we never see beyond the stereotype to the truth?

Elsewhere in Scripture, the devil is described as a roaring lion (1 Pet. 5:8), cunning (2 Cor. 11:3), and powerful (Jude 9). But before the Bible tells us any of this, we see the original story of sin in the opening pages of the Bible. In fact, Satan tells the first lie in the world.

The First Lie

Read Genesis 3:1-7.

What lie did Satan ask Adam and Eve to believe? Why was it a lie?

How did Satan's empty promises fail Adam and Eve? What were the immediate results of their sin?

Satan's tactics are shrewd, but they aren't new. He's been using the same schemes since the first moments of creation. God told Adam and Eve if they ate from the tree in the middle of the garden of Eden, they would die. Satan slithered up to them, and bald-faced lied. He said, "If you eat from the fruit, you will not surely die." Instead, he promised that eating the fruit would bring life. They believed the lie, disobeyed God, and death entered into the story of humanity.

Consider your own life. What has happened in your heart and in your conscience when you pursued something you knew was wrong?

What lies did you believe that prompted you to make that poor decision?

Satan is not stupid. He's quite the opposite—he's brilliant. And though he knows there will come a day when he will be destroyed forever, until then, he's going to inflict as much damage as he can. What tactics will he use to attempt to bring destruction to your life? Make no mistake, he will lie to you just as he did Adam and Eve. Believing his lies only brings devastation and death. Romans 1 paints a vivid picture of what happens in our lives when we embrace the lie of sin.

The Effects of the Lie

Read Romans 1:25-32.

According to the Scriptures, what happens when we exchange the truth about God for a lie?

When we reject God and trust our own judgment who are we really worshiping?

Romans 1 puts a mirror to our own experience. Paul writes that all sin means exchanging the truth about God for a lie (v. 25) then all kinds of pain and destruction follows (vv. 26-32). This passage communicates a sobering truth: when we choose our way over our Father's we are worshiping ourselves.

These verses restate what we will see in the parable of the prodigal son. Satan isn't mentioned in the parable, but if you listen closely you can hear the whisper of the father of lies in the young man's ear: "Hey, you're really missing out by living with your dad. Don't you think life would be more fulfilling if you lived by your own rules? Do you see that big city over there? That's where *real* life is happening." Every day we are tempted just like the young man in our story, to exchange the truth about our heavenly Father for a lie.

Where are you currently exchanging the truth about God for a lie?

Read 1 John 1:9. What hope is there for those of us who have embraced a lie?

Thankfully, there is a simple way to overcome a lie—believe the truth. Several centuries ago Martin Luther put it this way:

> *And though this world, with devils filled, should threaten to undo us,*
> *We will not fear, for God hath willed His truth to triumph through us;*
> *The Prince of Darkness grim, we tremble not for him;*
> *His rage we can endure, for lo, his doom is sure,*
> *One little word shall fell him.*[1]

1. www.hymnal.net/en/hymn/h/886

End your time by meditating on this truth—though we are attacked by the father of lies everyday, one simple truth can undo all the effects of His lies. We're going to look at this more closely in the next study.

Personal Study 2
The Truth

When we are in preschool we learn opposites. Up and down. Inside and outside. Loud and quiet. You might feel a little bit silly reading simple ideas from a toddler's books. However, if you remember those days, or have ever had a young child of your own, you know one of the first moral ideas a child learns is the opposite of a lie is the truth.

Sin is such a pervasive problem that we often can't see the simple solution for the ongoing sin in our life. Lies can be overcome with the truth. In order to combat the lies of the devil, we must believe the truth about God. Today we're going to look at two examples from the Bible to illustrate this point.

Exceptional Belief

Read Matthew 8:5-13.

What did Jesus find surprising about the Roman soldier's faith?

The soldier believed Jesus solely on His word. Why does the Roman soldier's faith seem like the exception instead of the rule?

Notice what happened in this passage; the soldier simply believed Jesus. He believed that if Jesus said the words—it was going to happen. This is incredible considering the Roman soldier didn't grow up in a Jewish home and he wasn't taught about God growing up. God is honored when His people believe Him. It's the simplest definition of a word that is used all the time in Scripture. It's called faith. Faith means we believe what God says.

Is there an area in your life where you simply need to believe what God says? If so, spend a few moments writing a prayer asking God to help you trust Him.

Believe in Me Also

The account in Matthew 8 shows us that even though the Jews were taught to believe God, they had a harder time than a non-Jewish soldier. If you ever find yourself doubting what God has said, know that you are not alone and you will find good company in Jesus' disciples. Thomas needed to see Jesus' hands (John 20:25). Peter denied Christ three times (John 18:27). Sometimes when Jesus' disciples doubted him, He rebuked them, but just as often He comforted them.

Read John 14:1-6.

What reason did Jesus give for His disciples to trust Him?

Compare what Jesus says about Himself in John 14:6 with what He said about Satan a few chapters earlier in John 8:44.

Jesus	Satan

Why should it be a comfort to us that Jesus sought to give His disciples comfort?

When we are tempted to doubt God and embrace the lie, why do we choose the lie instead of Jesus who invites us to trust Him?

Thinking about what it means to embrace the truth, we have to acknowledge we often fail. One of the blessings of studying the story of the prodigal son is it gives us the chance to consider the ways the prodigal failed without failing ourselves.

Satan is an expert at deception. He's the greatest deceiver in the history of the world and he's a master at presenting to us a picture of a better, fuller life apart from God. But even when we take the bait, God's Word is still true. This Bible study exists in part because of a sincere belief that in order to resist the lies we need to constantly be filling ourselves with truth.

Finding Truth

Read 2 Timothy 3:16-17.

What did Paul say the Bible is able to do for us?

When Paul wrote that the Bible is inspired or as some translations say "breathed out by God" it means that the words in the Bible are God's own words. How does having a book filled with God's words of truth help us combat the lies of the devil?

If you are a regular Bible reader, what difference do you notice in your life when you spend time reading the Bible compared to when you don't?

God gave us the Bible to lead us into truth. John 14 teaches us that truth is a person and His name is Jesus. For those of us who, like the prodigal, are tempted to wander from our Father's house, Jesus is telling us that we have a place in His Father's house if we place our faith in Him. He will show us the way as we rely on Him and daily seek His guidance in the Scriptures..

If you are new to the Bible or Christianity, the Bible reading plan in this book is meant to give you a simple way to read the Bible and discover what God is saying. If you haven't made a habit of Bible reading, would you commit to trying out the plan in this book?

End your time by reading Psalm 119:105. Pray that God will use this study and more importantly His Word to lead you to His truth.

Your word is a lamp to my feet
And a light to my path.
PSALM 119:105

Reading Plan

Genesis 3:1-24

Sin entered the world when Adam and Eve chose to believe a lie about God's character and nature. We lie to ourselves when we embrace sin.

Read Read the passage slowly and carefully with an open heart, asking the Holy Spirit to give you words of encouragement, direction, and correction.

Examine Pick a few verses and look at them more closely to gain a deeper understanding of what the Bible is saying.

Apply Consider how you will live differently in light of what you read.

Pray Pray through the passage and your application, asking God to change your heart and to change your life, based on the time you've spent in God's Word.

Reading Plan

Romans 5:1-21

Paul uses Adam as a starting point and explains how his sin spread throughout all of humanity. But even though our sin is great, the grace of Jesus is bigger.

Read   Read the passage slowly and carefully with an open heart, asking the Holy Spirit to give you words of encouragement, direction, and correction.

Examine   Pick a few verses and look at them more closely to gain a deeper understanding of what the Bible is saying.

Apply   Consider how you will live differently in light of what you read.

Pray   Pray through the passage and your application, asking God to change your heart and to change your life, based on the time you've spent in God's Word.

Reading Plan
Romans 1:18-28

Spend time together truly contemplating the effects of sin.

Read
Read the passage slowly and carefully with an open heart, asking the Holy Spirit to give you words of encouragement, direction, and correction.

Examine
Pick a few verses and look at them more closely to gain a deeper understanding of what the Bible is saying.

Apply
Consider how you will live differently in light of what you read.

Pray
Pray through the passage and your application, asking God to change your heart and to change your life, based on the time you've spent in God's Word.

Reading Plan

Ephesians 2:1-10

Sin is serious and its effects are widespread, but all who turn to Jesus in repentance and faith can find freedom for the reign of sin.

Read   Read the passage slowly and carefully with an open heart, asking the Holy Spirit to give you words of encouragement, direction, and correction.

Examine   Pick a few verses and look at them more closely to gain a deeper understanding of what the Bible is saying.

Apply   Consider how you will live differently in light of what you read.

Pray   Pray through the passage and your application, asking God to change your heart and to change your life, based on the time you've spent in God's Word.

Week 3
The Step

Start

Welcome to Session 3. Use these questions to get the conversation started.

Last week we took a deeper look into the lie that our best life is found outside the love of our heavenly Father. What was the most helpful takeaway from your personal study?

Our biggest missteps don't happen all at once, they're usually the result of a series of bad decisions. Take lying to your parents for example. Before you tell a lie, you have to determine there is some truth worth covering. Thinking about lying isn't wrong, lying is. To speak a lie into existence requires a step.

Every sin has a beginning. On the front end, sin always looks enticing, fun, satisfying and pleasurable. But sin will always take you to places you never intended to go. Last week we considered the origin of sin, this week, we will look at what happens when we take the step into sin.

Share about a mistake you made growing up. Was there a process that led to your mistake or did it happen all at once?

Ask someone to read 2 Samuel 11:1-4.

Pray and ask God to use our time together.
After praying, watch the video teaching

Watch

Use this section to take notes as you watch video session 3.

Video sessions available at lifeway.com/ProdigalSon
or with a subscription to smallgroup.com

Discuss

After viewing the video, discuss the following questions with your group.

The story of David and Bathsheba is not a parable that was told to make a point. It really happened. However, like the prodigal son, this account allows us to live vicariously through David and trace the process of sin in his life in the hope that we might avoid the same devastating choices.

> How does the progression from temptation to sin play out in David's life in 2 Samuel 11:1-4?

First, David was at home when he should've been at battle with his soldiers.

> What are some ways that we put ourselves into situations where we are more likely to enter into sin?

Next, David saw a beautiful woman, Bathsheba, bathing across the way. Seeing an attractive woman is not a sin. But what happened next was—David inquired who the woman was, discovered she was married, and still asked his men to go and get her. David used his power to sleep with Bathsheba and have her husband murdered.

> At what point did David take the step beyond temptation into sin? What is the difference between temptation and sin?

> Why is it beneficial to be familiar with the things that most tempt us?

> How does the lie of sin convince us that embracing our temptation is worth the risk? If you are comfortable, share an example from your own life.

> What are some things we could do to stop temptation in our lives before it gives birth to sin? How can other Christians help us here?

Close your discussion with prayer. Remind those in your group to complete the personal studies and Bible reading over the next week.

Personal Study 1

Anatomy of a Fall

So far we've talked about how the prodigal son has become convinced there is a better life for him outside of the love of his father. But before we continue on our journey with the prodigal, let's take a closer look at what causes us to make the decision to turn our backs on our heavenly Father and walk away.

Every sin starts with a first step. We've already seen how Satan loves to deceive us into believing there is happiness outside of the love of the Father. Now let's dig a little deeper into the deceptive nature of sin by turning to the letter of James where he urges us to overcome temptation by remembering the goodness of God.

Temptation

Read James 1:12-15.

According to James, where does temptation come from? Where does it not come from? Why are these important distinctions to make?

James connects temptations to trials. How do our temptations often come out of our trials?

We can't see inside the mind of the prodigal, so we can't know for certain what made him decide to walk away from his father's house. Jesus doesn't tell us. However, James teaches us that our temptations are often related to our trials. For instance, if you are experiencing financial difficulty, you might be tempted to steal. If you are lonely, you might struggle with seeking company in inappropriate relationships.

Yet, James is clear on one point; God never tempts us. God is never at fault when we walk away from Him and choose sin. While it's true that God does test us, He always does so to strengthen our faith, never to tempt us to sin. Sin is always our choice. We fall into the allure of sin, because sin is enticing.

The Allure of Sin

Why is it helpful for us to realize sin is "alluring"?

What does it mean to be "carried away" or "enticed" by our own lust (v 14)? When have you seen this process play out in your own experience?

"Alluring" isn't a word you hear very often. It means "powerfully and mysteriously attractive or fascinating; seductive."[1] James is creating a picture of a fish who is attracted to a lure in the water, but the fish is unaware that the lure will actually kill it. Temptation becomes a problem when it entices us into sin, because just like the fish, when sin reels us in, death is always waiting at the other end of the line.

What lies must we believe before we give in to temptation?

How has experience taught you that temptation is misleading and never delivers on its promise?

A fish wouldn't take the bait if it realized the inevitable outcome. When Christians embrace temptation, they have forgotten that sin leads to death. They were enticed by the promise of life where there was only death. God is the only One who can deliver on every promise, and He does every time. We've already seen that God doesn't tempt us, now let's look at what God does.

Grace in Temptation

Read James 1:16-18

According to these verses, what can God give us that temptation and sin never can?

Why should this be an encouragement to not succumb to temptation?

James contrasts the emptiness of temptation with the goodness of God. When Satan tempts us, he is hoping that we believe the lie that embracing temptation leads to blessing. But temptation is always a bait and switch. James tells us every good thing comes from God. Paul stated it more directly.

> *For the wages of sin is death, but the free gift of God*
> *is eternal life in Christ Jesus our Lord.*
> ROMANS 6:23

Sin always brings death and God always brings life—the kind of full and abundant life that is worth having. With Jesus there is no bait and switch, but only grace, love, and life. Jesus delivers on every promise

How did James refer to the people he was writing to in verse 16?
How can we prevent ourselves from being deceived?

In verse 16, James addresses the church. In fact, the entire New Testament was written to the church—a group of people seeking to follow Jesus together. Temptation and sin isolates us from God and from other people. And that is exactly what Satan wants. God intends for His children to live in biblical community. We're meant to wrestle with our temptations together. Imagine what might have been different for the prodigal if he had a wise friend able to provide good advice.

With which friends can you be honest about your temptations and struggles?

Look up James 5:16. Why should we desire the kind of relationships where we can share our struggles and sins with one another?

End your time today being honest about your temptations. Write them down below. Then make time to talk to someone about your struggles.

1. New Oxford American Dictionary.

End today by asking God to deliver you from your temptations, knowing that He will provide a way out.

No temptation has overtaken you but such as is common to man; and God is faithful, who will not allow you to be tempted beyond what you are able, but with the temptation will provide the way of escape also, so that you will be able to endure it.
1 CORINTHIANS 10:13

Personal Study 2

David's Great Sin(s)

In the previous personal study, we took a closer look at what James has to teach us about temptation. We saw how temptation invites us to take a first step into sin which will lead us into struggle, misery, and ultimately death. Today we're going to turn our attention to the life of David and the consequences of his sin.

Taking the Leap

Slowly read 2 Samuel 11:1-27 then answer the following questions.

Where in this passage do we see David being tempted?

At what points did David's temptations turn into sin?

After the initial sin, what additional sins did David commit in an attempt to cover the first sin?

At what points could David have resisted these temptations?

In the New American Standard Bible, the heading over 2 Samuel 11 reads, "Bathsheba, David's Great Sin." This title is memorable, but it's misleading. David's adultery with Bathsheba was one sin among many. David succumbed to temptation and sinned in numerous ways.

Initially, David remained at home while his men engaged in battle. David wasn't where he should've been and this created the opportunity for David to see Bathsheba on a nearby roof top. At this point, David's life spirals into a cycle of temptation and sin. From lust to adultery to deceit and murder—David's life veers further and further off track. The chapter ends with this sobering commentary:

> *The thing that David had done was evil in the sight of the LORD.*
> 2 SAMUEL 11:27

This series of events defined the rest of David's life and he was confronted with a variety of consequences. The kingdom David ruled was plagued with wars and he was betrayed by family (see 2 Sam. 15-19). David's life never quite returned to what it was before that night on the rooftop.

Imagine if the elderly David could speak to the younger David that night on the roof. What do you think he would say?

Before committing a sin, we often believe the lie that what we're entertaining is "no big deal." How does this story demonstrate there is no such thing as a small sin?

If the elderly David could speak to his younger self considering the false promise of temptation he would surely grab that young man by the shoulders, pull him close to his face, and plead with him to go home alone. He would warn that the momentary pleasure David was seeking would set into motion a series of events he would never recover from. He would tell the young David every step into sin is really a leap into death. Death of purity, death of integrity, death of trust, death of the abundant life that God has promised.

Looking Inward

If you know Jesus, you never read the Scriptures alone; the Holy Spirit is present with you, guiding you into all truth (John 16:13). Because of this reality, when we read David's account, we're not just reading about the sin in David's life, we're also being confronted with the presence of sin in our own life.

The point of this next exercise is not to reopen old wound or introduce fresh shame, but to help you see that David's experience with sin and temptation isn't an isolated incident. Instead, it's an example we can learn from that point us to Jesus (1 Cor 10:11). David was a man after God's own heart (1 Sam. 13:14). If he can so easily slip into sin, we can too. So let's take a look at our own lives.

Identify a past sin in your own life.
What temptation(s) did you experience before succumbing to this sin?

What lie did you believe that led you to think it was a good idea?

How did that sin fail to deliver on its promises?

If you could go back and talk to your previous self before you committed the sin, what would you say?

How does David's sin and temptation help you see your own sin and temptation more clearly? What lessons from David's story can you apply to your situation?

The goal of asking ourselves painful questions like the ones on the previous page is to shine a light into our own darkness. If you keep reading in 2 Samuel you will find that David was confronted about his sin by the prophet Nathan (2 Sam. 12). It took some encouragement, but David admitted his fault and sought restoration (Ps 51). We need to heed the wisdom we find in David's example.

Maybe this exercise hit a little too close to home and you are standing at that same crossroads where David and the prodigal stood—the crossroads of temptation and sin. Ignore the lying whispers of your enemy and choose to believe the words of your Savior. There is no future or abundant life to be found on the roof top across the way or in a faraway land. Stay at home.

End your time today by searching your own heart.

If there are ongoing sins for which you need to be forgiven, confess them to God, ask Him to forgive you, and receive the freedom from sin that only He can give.

If the sin you described is a thing of the past, thank Jesus for delivering you, and pray that He would protect you from stepping into sin in the future.

Reading Plan

2 Samuel 12:1-15

After David sinned with Bathsheba, God sent the prophet Nathan to confront and rebuke David.

Read Read the passage slowly and carefully with an open heart, asking the Holy Spirit to give you words of encouragement, direction, and correction.

Examine Pick a few verses and look at them more closely to gain a deeper understanding of what the Bible is saying.

Apply Consider how you will live differently in light of what you read.

Pray Pray through the passage and your application, asking God to change your heart and to change your life, based on the time you've spent in God's Word.

Reading Plan

2 Samuel 12:16-31

David responds to Nathan's correction with genuine sorrow and mourning as he feels the weight of his sin.

Read — Read the passage slowly and carefully with an open heart, asking the Holy Spirit to give you words of encouragement, direction, and correction.

Examine — Pick a few verses and look at them more closely to gain a deeper understanding of what the Bible is saying.

Apply — Consider how you will live differently in light of what you read.

Pray — Pray through the passage and your application, asking God to change your heart and to change your life, based on the time you've spent in God's Word.

Reading Plan
Proverbs 2:1-22

Avoiding sin requires wisdom which can be gained from God's Word. In this chapter, Solomon compares sin to an adulterous woman.

Read   Read the passage slowly and carefully with an open heart, asking the Holy Spirit to give you words of encouragement, direction, and correction.

Examine   Pick a few verses and look at them more closely to gain a deeper understanding of what the Bible is saying.

Apply   Consider how you will live differently in light of what you read.

Pray   Pray through the passage and your application, asking God to change your heart and to change your life, based on the time you've spent in God's Word.

Reading Plan

Proverbs 4:1-27

Solomon gives wisdom in the form of advice from a father to a son.

Read   Read the passage slowly and carefully with an open heart, asking the Holy Spirit
to give you words of encouragement, direction, and correction.

Examine   Pick a few verses and look at them more closely to gain a deeper understanding
of what the Bible is saying.

Apply   Consider how you will live differently in light of what you read.

Pray   Pray through the passage and your application, asking God to change your heart
and to change your life, based on the time you've spent in God's Word.

Week 4

The Consequences

Start

Welcome to Session 4. Use these questions to get the conversation started.

Last week we looked at what happened as King David fell into sin. How was looking at David's life helpful as you examined past sins and current temptations you're facing?

No one would choose to do something wrong if they knew what lay at the end of their decision. The prodigal would have never asked his father for his inheritance if he understood the consequences that awaited him on his journey. Before he requested his inheritance, the far country beamed with the promises of a better life.

A couple of weeks ago, we watched as the prodigal took that fateful first step down the path towards sin and rebellion in a distant land. This week we're going to take a look at what he found waiting for him at the end of the road. This session is about the consequences of our sin and rebellion.

What is the most memorable or humorous punishment you received growing up?

Ask someone to read Luke 15:13-16.

Pray and ask God to use our time together.
After praying, watch the video teaching.

Watch

Use this section to take notes as you watch video session 4.

Video sessions available at lifeway.com/ProdigalSon
or with a subscription to smallgroup.com

Discuss

After viewing the video, discuss the following questions with your group.

Why does it often take us going our own way before we realize the folly of our actions? What keeps us from heeding warnings along the way?

Jesus wasted no time revealing the consequences of the prodigal's decision. The young man took his father's gift and squandered it on "loose living." The language here communicates that the man took all he was given and threw all his possessions to the wind. He was broke and unfulfilled.

When have you or someone you know found themselves in a similar situation? When we pursue the far country, what is it that we're really searching for?

Why does sin always leaving us feeling impoverished?

Matt taught that Ecclesiastes 3:11 gives us a clue into what the prodigal (and we) hoped to find in the far country. All of us are searching for fulfillment that can only be found in God. Sin will always leave us broken and unfulfilled.

Read Ecclesiastes 3:11 together.

How have you observed this verse to be true in your experience?

If we all have this void in our lives without Jesus, what are some ways people try and fill this void even without realizing it?

What are some practical ways we can help people identify their true longing for eternity?

After discussion, close the session with prayer. Remind your group to complete the personal studies and Bible reading over the next week.

Personal Study 1
The Beautiful Mirage of Excess

This week we read about the consequence of taking a journey to a far country. Jesus wants us to see once and for all that sin is a dead-end road. This young man took the journey to the faraway land hoping to find fun and joy and the fullness of life, but when the party was over, he woke up broke, hungry, and covered in slop.

Over and over again, throughout the entirety of Scripture, the Bible makes a radical claim: The fullest and most satisfying expression of life can only be found in a relationship with God through Jesus Christ. That statement is shocking to many people in our culture, but the Bible goes on to teach an even more radical claim; all of us instinctively know that true life is found in relationship with God. The Bible teaches that all of us have an inner longing for "eternity."

> [God] has made everything appropriate in its time. He has also
> set eternity in their heart, yet so that man will not find out the
> work which God has done from the beginning even to the end.
> ECCLESIASTES 3:11

When do you first remember feeling this longing for eternity in your own heart?

God hardwires all of us to long for eternity because He wants us to find life in Him. God determines where we live, what we do, and who we know, in order that we might trace the evidence back to the eternal source (Acts 17:24-28). In His grace, God has placed markers all around us that point to Him—the Maker.

However, the prodigal son shows us a problem we all face. All of us pursue the markers and miss the Maker. The book of Ecclesiastes tackles this problem head on.

The Vanity of Success

Read Ecclesiastes 2:1-11.

Look through these verses and identify all the things that Solomon sought in hopes that it would fulfill him?

How does Solomon's list compare with the things people seek today to make them happy?

What was the result of Solomon's experiment of trying to find satisfaction in these things (see verse 11)?

After David died God chose David's son, Solomon, to rule in his place. As great as David was, Solomon was greater. He was the wisest man who ever lived and one of the wealthiest. Under his leadership, Israel expanded and prospered. He had it all, but all that he had blinded him from seeing what really mattered. His desire for the things of this world robbed his heart from God. No amount of pleasure, laughter, knowledge, property, servants, money, or esteem could satisfy him. Instead of fulfillment, his prosperity left him feeling empty

Thus I considered all my activities which my hands had done and the labor which I had 1exerted, and behold all was 2avanity and striving after wind and there was no profit under the sun.
ECCLESIASTES 2:11

Most scholars believe that Solomon wrote Ecclesiastes near the end of his life when he found, like the prodigal, that the best and most fulfilling life is not found in what our culture prizes. The whole point of the book of Ecclesiastes is the claim that nothing in all of the world, can meet and satisfy the deepest longings of the human heart. The best the world has to offer can never produce in us the happiness our hearts long for, because that type of happiness can only come from God.

Like the prodigal, Solomon came by this wisdom the hard way.

The Most Miserable Person in the World

Read 1 Kings 11:1-13 and compare it with Luke 15:13-16.

What consequences did Solomon and the prodigal suffer by pursuing the best they thought life had to offer?

Though you may not have failed as publicly as Solomon and the prodigal, when have you felt the consequences of pursuing sin over God?

Though all people are hardwired with eternity in their hearts, not all people search for eternity in a way that they can find it. Those who don't know God do this all the time. But what happens when a Christian searches for fulfillment apart from God?

I want to answer with a bold claim:

*A Christian who is walking in unrepentant sin is
the most miserable person in the world.*

Obviously, this is a huge generalization—and to be clear—when someone who doesn't know God pursues sin—it definitely leads to misery. But the effects of sin on a believer are more consequential because their hearts have found the true source of contentment. They have traced the desire for eternity back to the source. Jesus said:

> *This is eternal life, that they may know You, the only*
> *true God, and Jesus Christ whom You have sent.*
> JOHN 17:3

Jesus is telling us that our longing for eternity is satisfied in Him and Him alone. When a Christian tries to replace his or her heart's desire—Jesus—with anything else, it will always result in misery. Our longing for eternity can never be satisfied with anything other that Jesus. He is the only path to everlasting life.

Are you currently seeking purpose and meaning in anything other than a relationship with Jesus? If so, where?

Do you know anyone who is reeling from the consequences of sin? How might you comfort them and point them back to the hope of Jesus?

End your time today thanking God for every spiritual blessing He has given you in Christ. Ask that he would help you pursue Him above all else.

Personal Study 2

True Blessing

Blessing According to Culture

What would you say is your greatest blessing? Why?

If you're a basketball fan, or even if you're not, you have likely heard the name Kevin Durant. After a one year stint at the University of Texas, KD, as he is popularly known, entered the NBA in 2007 as the second overall pick and began to distinguished himself from his peers.

At the end of the 2018-19 season, Durant had tallied a growing list of accomplishments including: two championships, one league MVP, ten all-star game appearances, Rookie of the Year, and two Olympic gold medals. Durant is consistently at the top of the league in jersey sales and has a contract with Nike for tens of millions of dollars. From the outside looking in, Durant seems like a guy who has it all.

Yet after Durant won his first championship, he confessed that he didn't find it fulfilling. Former player Steve Nash worked with Durant the summer after his first championship and said,"[Durant] was searching for what it all meant. He thought a championship would change everything and found out it doesn't. He was not fulfilled."[1] Durant dreamed of hoisting the Larry O'Brien trophy his whole life, so why did the experience not live up to the dream? Durant discovered championships aren't enough; we are designed for more.

True blessing cannot be found in earthly accomplishments. No achievement, enjoyment, or praise will ever make us feel complete. The best life is found by pursuing the life God desires for us. If that's true, what does that life look like?

Jesus described the life God desires for us in His most famous teaching, known as the "Sermon on the Mount." Jesus begins with a series of brief statements called "the Beatitudes" about what it means to be "blessed."

Blessing According to Jesus

Read Matthew 5:1-12.

What does Jesus mean when He uses the word "blessed"?

Make a list of what Jesus says is a blessed life?

How does what Jesus counts as blessing compare with what our culture counts as blessing?

Which of the Beatitudes do you find most countercultural? Why?

When you look closely at what Jesus is saying in the Beatitudes, you realize that Jesus is making a radical statement. He makes a series of statements beginning with the word "Blessed". The specific Greek word Jesus used carries with it the idea of the fullest expression of blessing and happiness a person can experience.

Jesus modeled this teaching after the poems of His culture. The first Beatitude (v. 3) and the sixth (v. 10) have the same reward—"theirs is the kingdom of heaven." By teaching this way, Jesus is making the point that all that comes in between describes the attitude of a "blessed" person. But that's where Jesus' teaching is radically countercultural. According to Jesus, what produces this radical blessing is quite different from what Jesus' culture and own counts as blessing.

According to Jesus, blessing is found when we are poor in spirit, mourning, gentle, desiring righteousness, merciful, pursing purity, making peace, and even when we are being persecuted and insulted. Let's take a closer look at what Jesus counts as a blessed life.

> What does it mean to be "poor in spirit" (v. 3)? How is this different than the way the prodigal (and most of us) live?

> Many in our culture believe that we are happiest when we "follow our heart." How does this compare with Jesus' teaching to be "pure in heart?" (v. 8)?

To be poor in spirit means to be humble before God, recognizing that we are entirely dependent upon Him. This idea stands in contrast to many in our culture, who like the prodigal, have decided that life is best lived on our own terms. As the prodigal learned, living life on our own terms only results in pain.

We are poor in spirit when we agree with God about our sin, and turn to Him for grace, and allow Him to purify our hearts. The word "pure" in verse 8 means "unmixed or undivided." So what Jesus is conveying is that a Christian can experience the greatest level of happiness when his or her heart is fully devoted to God and not divided by God and something else. And why is the Christian with an undivided heart so blessed? Jesus says, "They will see God".

Jesus is teaching us that when are hearts are pure, we experience the highest form of human happiness, because we actually experience the presence of God to the fullest. On the other hand, when our hearts are divided and we give part of our heart to some other person or possession, it hinders our experience of God's presence. So if the fullness of joy is found in God's presence, a divided heart will prevent you from experiencing that fullness.

How can God use your painful lessons as a reminder in the future?

Sin keeps you from meeting the deepest longings of your heart, because those longings can only be fulfilled in Jesus. Walking in sin will produce emptiness and misery every single time. But the good news is, that when a believer sins, that emptiness and misery will always serve as a reminder that there is a place, and a home, and a Person that will always take you back, restore you to wholeness and fill the deepest longings of your heart.

Some of you may be in that place today—and I want you to hear something. The emptiness you feel as a result of your sin is the kindness of God gently calling you home. Make no mistake, sin and its consequences are profound. But even in the midst of your sin, God is still at work. Sin's inability to satisfy your deepest longings is nothing more than the tender and beautiful whisper of God that there's more to this life than what you're experiencing. Ask God to help you see sin for what it is —vanity—and I promise you He will.

If you are following Jesus on His terms, how has that resulted in fulfillment and contentment?

How does the fulfillment you find in Jesus compare the to the fulfillment of earth bound accomplishments?

1. https://www.slamonline.com/nba/steve-nash-kevin-durant-not-fulfilled-after-first-warriors-championship/

End your time today confessing the ways you have pursued your own path at the expense of God's best in your life. If God is convicting you of sin, thank Him for pulling you back and leading you to find life in Him.

Reading Plan
Luke 15:11-24

At the halfway mark of our study, take another look at the prodigal son.

Read Read the passage slowly and carefully with an open heart, asking the Holy Spirit to give you words of encouragement, direction, and correction.

Examine Pick a few verses and look at them more closely to gain a deeper understanding of what the Bible is saying.

Apply Consider how you will live differently in light of what you read.

Pray Pray through the passage and your application, asking God to change your heart and to change your life, based on the time you've spent in God's Word.

Reading Plan

Romans 6:20-23

Paul highlights the consequences of sin against the gift of grace.

Read — Read the passage slowly and carefully with an open heart, asking the Holy Spirit to give you words of encouragement, direction, and correction.

Examine — Pick a few verses and look at them more closely to gain a deeper understanding of what the Bible is saying.

Apply — Consider how you will live differently in light of what you read.

Pray — Pray through the passage and your application, asking God to change your heart and to change your life, based on the time you've spent in God's Word.

Reading Plan
Matthew 6:19-24

Many abandon God to pursue worldly goods like money and possession. Jesus warned about the consequences of this pursuit in the Sermon on the Mount.

Read   Read the passage slowly and carefully with an open heart, asking the Holy Spirit to give you words of encouragement, direction, and correction.

Examine   Pick a few verses and look at them more closely to gain a deeper understanding of what the Bible is saying.

Apply   Consider how you will live differently in light of what you read.

Pray   Pray through the passage and your application, asking God to change your heart and to change your life, based on the time you've spent in God's Word.

Reading Plan

Ephesians 4:30-32

Walking in sin grieves the Holy Spirit and keeps us from experiencing the fullness of life available to us in Christ.

Read — Read the passage slowly and carefully with an open heart, asking the Holy Spirit to give you words of encouragement, direction, and correction.

Examine — Pick a few verses and look at them more closely to gain a deeper understanding of what the Bible is saying.

Apply — Consider how you will live differently in light of what you read.

Pray — Pray through the passage and your application, asking God to change your heart and to change your life, based on the time you've spent in God's Word.

Week 5

The Realization

Start

Welcome to Session 5. Use these questions to get the conversation started.

Last week we talked about how God has put eternity in the hearts of men (Ecc. 3:11). As you've processed this over the last week, how have you observed the statement to be true?

Last week we saw the prodigal at the end of his rope, impoverished, and tending to pigs. He learned that the lights of the far country were not as bright as he'd hoped. Everything he thought would bring him happiness had actually produced pain and misery he never could've imagined. The prodigal had a wake up called and realized he should've never left his father in the first place.

This week we're going to take a look at what happens in the life of a Christian when they realize they are living in sin and disobedience. This realization is a first step on our journey back to the father.

Describe a time you were wrong about something? What made you realize you were wrong?

Ask someone to read Luke 15:17.

Pray and ask God to use our time together.
After praying, watch the video teaching..

Watch

Use this section to take notes as you watch video session 5.

Discuss

After viewing the video, discuss the following questions with your group.

> Last week we talked about the consequences of our sin. How does feeling the weight of our sins lead us to turn back to the Father?

> When have you had a similar realization like the prodigal, that your sin wasn't worth it?

> Read Philippians 1:6. Why should this verse give wandering Christians the confidence to return to the Father?

> Read John 16:7-8. How does the Holy Spirit help us realize the folly of our sin?

If you know Jesus and are wandering in the far off country of sin, the good news is that you will always come to your senses. God cares too much about His work in your life to let you continue in sin. When we are tempted to sin, the Spirit of God convicts and urges us towards reconciliation with our Father.

Matt ended our time by addressing two groups—those considering sin and those stuck in a pattern of sin. Let's end our time considering these groups together.

> If you're in the first group, Matt mentioned that for a believer, sin is a "monumental waste of time." What did he mean by this? Why is this helpful to remember when we are considering entering into sin?

> Or, are you in the second group? Is there a sin you are dealing with that you need the people in this room to help you step away from?

Close your discussion with prayer. Remind those in your group to complete the personal studies and Bible reading over the next week.

Personal Study 1

God's Pursuit through Our Sin

What's the most helpful truth you've learned so far on our walk with the prodigal?

A Valid Question

This week we've crossed the halfway point on our walk with the prodigal. Here, our friend finds himself in a literal pigpen. The young man has fallen as far as a person can fall. He's abandoned his family, spent all of his inheritance on parties and prostitutes, and now finds himself in the worst situation of his life. A famine has come into the "faraway land," and he finds himself starving, dirty, broke, and filled with shame. In that moment, he comes to his senses.

> When he came to his senses, he said, 'How many of my father's hired workers have more than enough food, and here I am dying of hunger!
>
> LUKE 15:17

This leads to a valid and natural question; Have you ever wondered why God allows His children to sin in the first place? God's is all-knowing and all-powerful, right? At any point, when his sons and daughters are standing at the crossroads of temptation and sin, He could intervene. But as we saw in a previous week, sometimes it takes us tasting the bitter fruit of sin, for us to fully realize the sweetness of God's love.

Have you ever found yourself asking a similar question? How did you navigate the tension?

God's Work through the Pigpen

Have you ever had a moment like the prodigal when you realized the sin you were pursing wasn't delivering on its promises? If you're a Christian, if you haven't yet, you probably will. And yet, God is still at work. When it comes to His sons and daughters, while God may let us take a trip to the faraway land, He never lets us stay there—not forever (1 John 2:3-4). The apostle Paul wrote about this special grace of God in the midst of our sin: He wrote:

> *I am sure of this, that he who started a good work in you will carry it on to completion until the day of Christ Jesus.*
> PHILIPPIANS 1:6

Restate this verse in your own words.

How does it make you feel to know that God is always working and will not let His work in you run dry?

The church at Philippi was enduring a great deal of hardship from the culture around them. Unlike the prodigal, it was outside of their control. In their struggle, Paul reassured them, that no matter what, God would not stop working among them. He would take the good work going on in their lives and bring it to completion.

Philippians 1:6 is a promise that God's love for us is not circumstantial He loves all His children at all times. When they experience hardship as a result of sin, He is present and active in His care and affection

Why is this promise important for us to remember when we mess up?

What happens when we mistakenly believe that God's love is circumstantial like our love for one another is?

God is not like us, and that's a good thing. No matter what happens, God is always with us. He will never leave us or forsake us (Heb. 13:5). If you are in a redemptive relationship with Jesus, He will never stop working in your life. He doesn't give up, as we might, when the road is hard.

Paul's words were meant to comfort the Philippians and they're meant to comfort us. This verse is a promise that if you are truly God's son or daughter, He will never let you go. If you have walked down the path of sin, there are better, brighter days ahead of you. However, these words should also unsettle us because they contain a warning.

If God is truly concerned in finishing His work in us (and He is), how might we expect God to respond when we continue to run away from the life found in Him and into continued sin?

Because God is always at work in our lives, He will never sit idly by when His sons and daughters walk down the path of sin. While God is patient with us, He simply won't allow his children to continue down a road that will harm us. In his great love, He will come at us like a steamroller to bring us back home to Him. One of the best evidences that you are a child of God, is not that you never sin, but that you never continue in your sin. Why? God promises us He simply won't allow it.

In the next personal study, we will look at how God brings us back, but before we do that, let's consider how God has used our own realizations to shape our faith story.

Using Your Story

Have you ever found yourself in a moment of clarity and realization like the prodigal? Let's spend some time reflecting on it and see what we can learn from it.

When was your last "prodigal" moment? What happened? What made you come to your senses?

How is God using and redeeming the time you spent wandering?

How has time or distance given you some perspective on what happened?

Who needs to hear the story of what God did in your life? When will you tell them?

End today by asking God to use your story to help someone who needs to hear it.

Personal Study 2

How God Brings Us Back

Think about the times in your life when you've received correction from a parent, friend, or coworker. What kind of correction do you find most helpful?

In the last personal study, we saw that God will always complete the work He begins in the life of His sons and daughters. Throughout this study, we've seen the friction sin creates against God's work. Like anyone who cares for us, God will not let us persist in choices that are harmful. Because of His perfect care for us, He corrects us. Today we're going to look at the means God most often uses to call us back from the far-off country. The first means God uses is the Holy Spirit.

The Leading of the Holy Spirit

Read John 16: 7-8.

How is the Holy Spirit described here?

What role does the Holy Spirit play in the life of a believer?

How have you experienced the Holy Spirit's conviction "concerning sin and righteousness"?

At the moment someone trusts in Jesus, the Holy Spirit comes to live inside of them (see Rom. 8:11; 1 Cor. 3:16; Ezek 36:27). The Bible calls this "indwelling" because the Spirit is dwelling inside of us, helping us resist the lies of the devil and the lure of sin.

Read John 16:13-14.

How does Jesus describe the work of the Holy Spirit in these verses?

What is the ultimate goal of the Holy Spirit's work in our lives (v. 14)?

Followers of Jesus never struggle against sin alone, we have help from the Spirit of God. When the devil assaults us with lies of a better life, the Holy Spirit urges us to remember our identity as children of God (Rom. 8:16). When our eyes are set on sin, He gently reminds us: "That's not who you are. You were not created for this. Turn around, and come back home." The Holy Spirit leads us to glorify God.

Why are we more likely to sin when we forget that we are children of God?

What areas are you most tempted to find your identity outside of God?

Most sin originates from a fundamental misunderstanding of who we are—sons and daughters of God. When we forget that identity, we live out of a false understanding of ourselves and pursue plans that can never fulfill us. In those times, God's Spirit prompts us to remember who are in Jesus. But if we continue to resist the Spirit's urging, God will change tactics and remind us who we are by disciplining us as sons and daughters.

By Disciplining Us as Sons and Daughters

This week we have seen God is more committed to the work He began in our lives than we are. He desires for His children to continually become more and more like Jesus. Because of this desire, when we disobey and veer off toward the path of sin, God brings discipline to our lives which leaves us with no option but to come back home. God promises that He will discipline those He loves. And who does He love? He loves His sons and daughters.

Read Hebrews 12:5-8.

What is the difference between discipline and punishment?

Why do parents discipline their children?

Why is it important to note that God disciplines us *because* we are sons and daughters?

The author of Hebrews uses the word discipline intentionally. A good parent disciplines their child when he or she darts out into a crowded parking lot. Why? Because it's dangerous. A child runs because he or she is oblivious to the danger. The child needs discipline, not punishment, because discipline is corrective and punishment is punitive.

Like children who break free from their parents hand and rush into a parking lot, we lack the perspective to distinguish harmless fun from danger. We need correction. And like a good parent, God doesn't punish us; He disciplines us in order to lead us to a better path.

What happens if we disconnect the discipline of the Lord from our identity as children of God?

How does discipline prove that we are children of God? Have you ever learned this by experience? If so, how?

The father of lies would be thrilled if all God's children saw His corrective discipline as punishment. The book of Hebrews tells us that the presence of God's discipline in our lives proves that we are His children. God won't discipline someone else's child (see verse 8). God's never-ending, relentless pursuit of us is evidence that we are His. He loves us too much to let us continue in sin.

Is there anything in your life that would lead you to believe God is pursuing you through discipline right now?

Based on this week of study, how will you respond differently the next time you sense the discipline of the Lord in your life?

End your time together thanking God for the privilege of being God's child. Thank the Spirit that Paul's words are true of you.

For all who are being led by the Spirit of God, these are sons of God.
ROMANS 8:14

Reading Plan

Romans 8:5-11

For the believer, the Holy Spirit is always at work in our lives to help us realize our sins and lead us in righteousness.

Read   Read the passage slowly and carefully with an open heart, asking the Holy Spirit to give you words of encouragement, direction, and correction.

Examine   Pick a few verses and look at them more closely to gain a deeper understanding of what the Bible is saying.

Apply   Consider how you will live differently in light of what you read.

Pray   Pray through the passage and your application, asking God to change your heart and to change your life, based on the time you've spent in God's Word.

Reading Plan
Psalm 94:12-15

Notice how God uses discipline to guide His people back into a right relationship with Him.

Read   Read the passage slowly and carefully with an open heart, asking the Holy Spirit to give you words of encouragement, direction, and correction.

Examine   Pick a few verses and look at them more closely to gain a deeper understanding of what the Bible is saying.

Apply   Consider how you will live differently in light of what you read.

Pray   Pray through the passage and your application, asking God to change your heart and to change your life, based on the time you've spent in God's Word.

Reading Plan

Acts 9:1-19

Saul persecuted the church with zeal until Jesus Christ confronted him on the road to Damascus. Saul realized the depth of his mistake and found the comfort of Jesus.

Read   Read the passage slowly and carefully with an open heart, asking the Holy Spirit to give you words of encouragement, direction, and correction.

Examine   Pick a few verses and look at them more closely to gain a deeper understanding of what the Bible is saying.

Apply   Consider how you will live differently in light of what you read.

Pray   Pray through the passage and your application, asking God to change your heart and to change your life, based on the time you've spent in God's Word.

Reading Plan

Proverbs 3:11-12

When God disicplines us, it is evidence of His love and grace and His desire for us to be reconciled to Him.

Read   Read the passage slowly and carefully with an open heart, asking the Holy Spirit to give you words of encouragement, direction, and correction.

Examine   Pick a few verses and look at them more closely to gain a deeper understanding of what the Bible is saying.

Apply   Consider how you will live differently in light of what you read.

Pray   Pray through the passage and your application, asking God to change your heart and to change your life, based on the time you've spent in God's Word.

Week 6

The Speech

Start

Welcome to Session 6. Use these questions to get the conversation started.

Over the last week you were challenged to write out your own "coming to your senses" moment (pg. 79). What did you learn as you thought through this? Who might your story help?

In our time walking with the prodigal, we've seen the young man demand his inheritance, and head for the promise of a better life in a far off country. We've heard how he wasted all his father's fortune and ended up wishing he ate as well as the pigs he tended to. Most recently, we saw the prodigal realize he made a big mistake and resolved to head back home to his father. This week the prodigal wrestles with what he will say to his father when he returns.

What makes a good apology? What elements must be included?

On the other hand, how would you describe a bad apology?

Let's take a closer look at the speech the young prodigal prepared as he began his trek down the road home.

Ask someone to read Luke 15:18-19.

Pray and ask God to use our time together.
After praying, watch the video teaching.

Watch

Use this section to take notes as you watch video session 6.

Video sessions available at lifeway.com/ProdigalSon
or with a subscription to smallgroup.com

Discuss

Up until this point in the parable, we've only learned about the prodigal through what he does. These verses mark a shift in the story. As the son rehearses what he will say when he faces his father, we're granted access into his heart. The first line is a blueprint for biblical repentance.

Verse 18 is the first line of the speech. What has the prodigal realized about himself and his father?

Why does true repentance require admission of guilt to both God and others? Where do we see both in the prodigal's speech?

What are some excuses we make to minimize our responsibility when we're wrong? Why does making excuses negate our apology?

The son says: "Father, I have sinned against heaven and before you." He offers no deflection of his failure. Instead, he comes out and owns his sin against God and his father. True repentance involves a vertical aspect—admitting fault to God—and a horizontal aspect—admitting fault to others harmed.

Verse 19 is the second line of the speech. What is wrong with this statement? What has the son misunderstood about the love of his father?

When you seek God for forgiveness what does your "speech" look more like—the first line, the second, both? Explain.

Read Psalm 103:12. Why is it important for us to realize that the depth of our sin can never be greater than the love of Jesus? Why do we need to know this not only when we mess up, but every other day of our lives?

The prodigal's speech veered off the road when he said, "I am no longer worthy to be called your son." We can never sin so much that God won't accept us. Nothing can ever separate us from the love of God in Jesus.

Close your discussion with prayer. Remind your group to complete the personal studies and Bible reading over the next week.

Personal Study 1

Model Repentance

When was the last time you had to make a big apology? What elements did you include in that apology?

In our group study, we saw the speech the prodigal prepared on the way back to his father. You've probably had to come up with a similar speech at some point in your life—the one when you know you did something wrong and the time has come to admit it. Like the prodigal, you probably rehearsed the speech over and over again before delivering it.

We all know the basic outline—"I've messed up really bad and I hope that you will not give up on me." Sincere apologies take this shape because we all understand that true sorrow includes two elements—admitting fault and seeking restoration. As we saw, the prodigal nailed this basic outline:

> *Father, I have sinned against heaven, and in your sight*
> LUKE 15:18

These are the words of a truly repentant person. He doesn't start his speech with excuses as to why he sinned. He doesn't start his speech with all the ways the father let him down that led to his leaving in the first place. He doesn't offer any deflection of his failure at all—he just comes out and owns his sin. These words are reminiscent of another masterclass in repentance we find in Scripture.

Taking Ownership

Read Psalm 51:1-5.

What specific requests does David make in these verses?

How would you describe David's attitude? What let's us know that David is truly sorry as opposed to just being sorry that he got caught?

Why do we struggle with asking forgiveness from those we have wronged, or from God Himself?

Earlier in this study we looked at David's sin with Bathsheba. Psalm 51 is David's response to this specific sin. David's prayer shows genuine sorrow and heartfelt repentance before God. David confronts his sin and doesn't make excuses. He doesn't deflect the blame onto others. He owns 100 percent of the responsibility. David says, "For I know my transgressions." A person is truly repentant owns their sins against God and others.

Do you find it harder to apologize to God or to others? Why are both steps necessary?

True repentance always has a horizontal aspect (realizing your sin against others) and a vertical one (realizing you have sinned against God). Realizing you've sinned against another person is important. Realizing you've sinned against the perfectly Holy God of the universe is even more important.

David acknowledged God as the primary party offended by his sin. Why is our sin always ultimately against God?

Besides truly owning his own sin, David also realized that, first and foremost, he sinned against God. This is significant considering the number of people David had sinned against. The list is not short. He sinned against the nation of Israel by neglecting his kingly duties. He sinned against Bathsheba by lusting after her and calling his men to bring her to his room. He sinned against Uriah by taking his wife and then having him killed. And these are just the sins 2 Samuel 11 makes obvious to us. Yet in all of these sins, and in all of your sins, the most offended party is always God. He's God, and He's the one that ultimately established the standard of holiness He calls us to live out.

Do you see your sin the way David did—as against God?

Receiving Forgiveness

Read Psalm 51:6-12.

Once David admitted his sin, what changed about David's prayer?

What freedom have you found when you express your sin to God and others and ask for forgiveness?

Because God is the primary party offended by our sin, He is also the one with the power to restore and forgive us, which He will do every time. In these verses, the distance created between David and God because of his sin is quickly closing. As he confesses guilt and asks for restoration, you can feel David's heart drawing closer to God. David's prayer transforms into a series of requests for restoration and renewal. Receiving forgiveness from God changes the way we live.

Embracing Restoration

Read Psalm 51:13-19.

How does David plan to live differently as a result of the forgiveness he received?

Why should receiving forgiveness from God radically alter the way we live?

David saw the story of his failing and restorations as a means God could use to bring other people into a relationship with Him. He had a healthy understanding of repentance and forgiveness. The prodigal understood repentance, but had a little trouble receiving forgiveness.

In the next personal study, we're going to take a look at the second line of the prodigal's speech and think through a mistake we make all too often.

End today by thanking God for the forgiveness He's given you in Jesus. Use these words as a starting point:

Therefore there is now no condemnation for those who are in Christ Jesus.
ROMANS 8:1

Personal Study 2

The Radical Forgiveness of God

Have you ever sinned, failed, or messed up, either in a small or large way and that sin made you feel a palpable distance between you and God? It's common, because that's what sin does. It creates distance between us and God.

In the garden of Eden, before sin entered the picture, Adam and Eve had complete unhindered access to God. They could walk and talk and fellowship, face-to-face with God. But when they sinned they lost all of that because sin created a wedge between them and their perfectly holy Creator. While nothing can separate us from the love of God in Christ Jesus—our sin can create a sense of separation and make us question our relationship with God.

Have you ever felt that way? You probably have. What you need to know is that Satan loves to enter into space created by the feeling of separation and fill it with lies. He will do everything he can to nurture and grow your doubts until you are too ashamed to approach God. Today, we're going to consider truth from Scripture that will help us combat this lie from the devil.

If We Confess Our Sins

Read 1 John 1:9.

> *If we confess our sins, he is faithful and just to forgive us*
> *our sins and to cleanse us from all unrighteousness.*
> 1 JOHN 1:9 (ESV)

Practically speaking, what does it mean to confess our sins?

What does confession look like in the prodigal's speech in Luke 15:18?

Confession is the role that we play in regards to God's forgiveness. Confession is a word that means to "agree with." In other words, when we sin, we cognitively, emotionally, and verbally agree with God that what we have done is wrong and falls short of His glorious perfection.

The prodigal realized what he had done, agreed in his heart, and said with his mouth that what He did was wrong. He knew his father's house was better. When we confess our sins, we are acknowledging that God's way is better. Once we have done that, God takes over. The next part of the speech is where the prodigal, (and we) miss the mark in understanding God's forgiveness.

Why should this verse give you confidence in approaching God for forgiveness?

He is Faithful and Just to Forgive

Read the second line of the prodigal's speech in Luke 15:19 then reread 1 John 1:9. What did the prodigal miss about the forgiveness of God?

John states, "If we confess our sins, He is faithful and just to forgive us". The amazing thing about God is that while we are often unfaithful, He is always faithful. It's impossible for God to be unfaithful to what He promises. We are like the prodigal, we believe we are unfit to be God's son or daughter. Yet Scripture says, when we confess our sins, there will never be a time or a place or an instance when sin will cause God to be unfaithful in offering His forgiveness to us.

Many of us simply don't believe God is faithful to forgive. We wonder deep down inside if there's a limit to His forgiveness towards His children. But that could not be farther from the truth. He is faithful to forgive, every single time, and there is not a type or quota of sin that can shake or change that faithfulness.

For example, when many of us mess up, we say a prayer like this: "God, I'm so sorry, please forgive me, please have mercy on me". From there we go on to bargaining with God: "God, if you'll forgive me, I'll never do it again." When we do this, we are missing a crucial truth about God's character and put conditions on His forgiveness.

How do your own prayers reflect what you really believe about God's forgiveness?

What kind of conditions do you tend to place on God forgiving you?

Notice that Scripture doesn't say that "when we confess our sins God is faithful and merciful to forgive us if we promise to never do it again", it says that "God is faithful and just" to forgive our sins.

What does it mean for someone to be "just"?

What does it mean for God to be just in forgiving us?

God's justice in forgiving sin is a key concept that most of us simply haven't thought about in regards to God's forgiveness.

You see, when Christ came to this earth, He lived a perfect life and He never sinned. And so when God sent Jesus to the cross, He did that so Jesus' shed blood would be the once and for all-time payment for all of our sins. Not part of your sin. Not most of your sin. Not all of your sin except that really bad one you committed in high school. Jesus' blood is the only condition necessary for your forgiveness. When Jesus hung on the cross, battered, bleeding, and broken, He cried out, "It is finished!" If you are a Christian, your sin is finished; it was canceled by Jesus on the cross.

Maybe you've struggled believing that God could really forgive you. If you haven't, you probably know someone who has. Here's what you need to know; when we confess our sins to God, the Scripture says God is "just" to forgive us of our sins. For God not to forgive you, would be unjust. Why? Because all your sin was already paid for by Jesus. And for God to not forgive a sin that had already been paid for, would be the height of injustice—something that God is incapable of. Your God is a faithful and just God. Your sin has already and forever been paid for and His justice demands that He can never hold that sin against you. Now and forever.

> Who do you know that struggles believing that God can really forgive them? What might it look like to help them see the depth of forgiveness using 1 John 1:9?

> How will your prayers for forgiveness change based on what you've read today?

> End your time by praying that God would give you the opportunity to share His forgiveness with someone this week.

Reading Plan

Psalm 32:1-11

In addition to Psalm 51, this psalm highlights the blessing that comes from heartfelt repentance.

Read   Read the passage slowly and carefully with an open heart, asking the Holy Spirit to give you words of encouragement, direction, and correction.

Examine   Pick a few verses and look at them more closely to gain a deeper understanding of what the Bible is saying.

Apply   Consider how you will live differently in light of what you read.

Pray   Pray through the passage and your application, asking God to change your heart and to change your life, based on the time you've spent in God's Word.

Reading Plan

1 John 1:5-10

This week we studied 1 John 1:9. Read this whole section to develop a fuller appreciation of what John was writing.

Read   Read the passage slowly and carefully with an open heart, asking the Holy Spirit to give you words of encouragement, direction, and correction.

Examine   Pick a few verses and look at them more closely to gain a deeper understanding of what the Bible is saying.

Apply   Consider how you will live differently in light of what you read.

Pray   Pray through the passage and your application, asking God to change your heart and to change your life, based on the time you've spent in God's Word.

Reading Plan
Colossians 3:12-17

Once we have received radical forgiveness from God, it changes the way we live and interact with others.

Read Read the passage slowly and carefully with an open heart, asking the Holy Spirit to give you words of encouragement, direction, and correction.

Examine Pick a few verses and look at them more closely to gain a deeper understanding of what the Bible is saying.

Apply Consider how you will live differently in light of what you read.

Pray Pray through the passage and your application, asking God to change your heart and to change your life, based on the time you've spent in God's Word.

Reading Plan

1 Timothy 1:15-16

Every sinner, without qualification can receive forgiveness and live free from shame and guilt.

Read   Read the passage slowly and carefully with an open heart, asking the Holy Spirit to give you words of encouragement, direction, and correction.

Examine   Pick a few verses and look at them more closely to gain a deeper understanding of what the Bible is saying.

Apply   Consider how you will live differently in light of what you read.

Pray   Pray through the passage and your application, asking God to change your heart and to change your life, based on the time you've spent in God's Word.

Week 7
The Return

Start

Welcome to Session 7. Use these questions to get the conversation started.

In last week's personal study, you were challenged to think of someone who needed to know that God is faithful and just to forgive them of all their sin.

Who came to mind?

How did it benefit you to dwell upon that idea yourself?

The prodigal has taken off to a faraway land, been impoverished by sin, and has prepared a speech to beg his father's forgiveness. He's on the way home.

This week, as the prodigal continues on the road home, we will deal with some of the barriers we build up in our minds and hearts that keep us from coming home to God, where we can be unhindered by guilt and shame.

Have you ever put off doing something that you needed to do for longer than you should? What kept you from moving forward?

Ask someone to read Luke 15:20.

Pray and ask God to use our time together.
After praying, watch the video teaching.

Watch

Use this section to take notes as you watch video session 7.

Video sessions available at lifeway.com/ProdigalSon
or with a subscription to smallgroup.com

Discuss

After viewing the video, discuss the following questions with your group.

Notice how Jesus describes the prodigals goal. Jesus could've said he arose and came "home" or he could've said he arose and came "to his village", but He didn't. Jesus said the prodigal "arose and came to his father." That phrase is intentional. His father *was* home to him, just as for all children of God— our heavenly Father is home to us.

> Do you see God as being "home" to you? Why is this a helpful way to view our relationship with the Father?

For a child of God, no person or place in the entire world can ever be home except in fellowship with God. But as Matt discussed in the video teaching, there are two barriers that keep children of God from going back home. The first barrier is taking sin too seriously.

> Why is it so easy to believe the lie our sin is too great for God to overcome?

> How might believing this lie trap us in a cycle of repeated sin?

> Read Romans 5:20-21. How does realizing that God's grace is greater than our sin help readily turn to our Father when we step into sin?

The second barrier is that we do not take sin seriously enough.

> Read Matthew 5:4. What is the difference between mourning your sin and taking it too seriously?

> Read 2 Corinthians 5:21. How does the cross help us understand the cost of our sin?

> How will adequately mourning our sin keep us from being the kind of person who take repeated trips to the far off country?

Close your discussion with prayer. Remind those in your group to complete the personal studies and Bible reading over the next week.

Personal Study 1

Embrace the Love of God

As we pick up our story again, the prodigal's sin has left him impoverished. He's prepared a speech to beg his father's forgiveness, and he's finally stepped out of the pigpen and taken those first steps to return home. In today and tomorrow's personal studies, we will deal with two of the barriers that keep us from coming home to God and living with Him, unhindered by guilt and shame. We'll consider the first today.

One of the primary lessons we learn from the story of the prodigal is the inexhaustible love of God. Many prodigals fear returning home because they fail to understand the inexhaustible love God has for them. Far more Christians than we realize spend time asking questions like, "How could God love somebody that keeps failing Him?"

If you're honest, do you ever struggle believing God loves you? Why?

Doubting God's love for us often originates from a false belief that our sin is greater than God's love for us. Consider this example; you sin and step outside the bounds of God's best for your life, but instead of turning back to God, you continue to rebel. You continue to stray from God, not because you want to continue sinning, but because you believe your failure has caused an irreparable breach in your relationship.

Thankfully, God is not like us; there will never be an uncorrectable breach in our relationship with Him because it's simply not possible to out sin God's love for us. God takes away our sin and uses all of our experiences—including our failures—to bring us closer to Himself.

How Can God Use Our Sin?

Read Romans 8:28-30.

Fill in the blank based on your reading: God causes _____ _____ to work together for good (Rom. 8:28).

To be clear, sin is always wrong, but it is never so severe that it will permanently hinder our relationship with God. One of the fascinating things about God is He intentionally allows His children to wrestle and struggle with certain parts of their walk with Him. Like a toddler learning to walk, progress takes time and multiple failures before growth occurs. The good news for us is that God is able to use "all things"—the good, the bad, and everything in between—for His glory.

Look at verses 28-30 again. What process does Paul outline for growth?

How have your failures led to a process of growth in your life?

In Romans 8, Paul is saying that God has a plan for His children that never ceases. Paul says God has "predestined" or planned the lives of those who love Him (v. 29). As followers of Jesus, our entire life is a process where God conforms (makes us more like) Jesus. No failure on our part can thwart this work of God in our lives, because God's plan is not dependent upon us. The plan begins with God before we are born and continues through our natural life until the time we enter into eternity (v. 30).

How have your failures caused you to grow in a way that your successes couldn't?

Think about it, if God made you perfect on the day you came to know Jesus, then you'd never again have to depend on Him. Instead of instant perfection, God allows us to have a journey of ups and downs, successes and failures, highs and lows, all with the intended design to keep us on a lifelong path of dependence and discovery of His unimaginable grace. It's often in those seasons of hardship and struggle that God teaches us lessons that stick and make the greatest impact on our souls. And it's through those seasons of struggle and restoration that God shows us how He deals with our sin.

What Does God Do with our Sin?

The Bible is filled with illustrations of how He deals with our sin.

Read the following verses and underline God's actions.

As far as the east is from the west,
So far has He removed our transgressions from us.
PSALM 103:12

For You have cast all my sins behind Your back.
ISAIAH 38:17

For I will forgive their iniquity, and their sin I will remember no more.
JEREMIAH 31:34

He will again have compassion on us;
He will tread our iniquities under foot.
Yes, You will cast all their sins
Into the depths of the sea
MICAH 7:19

Having canceled out the certificate of debt consisting of
decrees against us, which was hostile to us; and He has
taken it out of the way, having nailed it to the cross.
COLOSSIANS 2:14

How does your perspective on your sin as a follower of Jesus compare to God's?

If God doesn't remember our sins, why can't we stop thinking about them?

How does the cross help us see both the severity of sin and also the depth of mercy and grace side by side?

God has taken our sins and taken them as faraway from us as possible. He has cast it away, trampled over it and forgotten it. He took your sin, laid it upon Jesus, and expressed all of His judgment against sin on the cross. If you know Jesus, your sin is no problem for God. In fact, He can't even remember it!

If you are God's child, no matter how many times you've let go of Him, He will never let go of you. You can never out sin God's love. He is always ready to receive those who return to Him.

End your time today by praying through the verses on the previous page, thanking God for fully removing your sin against Him. Commit to live in the forgiveness God have given you.

Personal Study 2

Mourn Your Sin

How would you describe your typical response to sin in your life? Grief, sorrow, ambivalence? Why?

The Other Brother

In the previous personal study, we examined one barrier that keeps us from coming home to God—we take our sin too seriously. While many of us struggle believing the grace of God, many others swing to the opposite end of the spectrum—they fail to take their sin seriously enough. That's really what's going on with a character in the story of the prodigal son that we haven't talked about—the older brother. He's the brother who stayed home, stayed faithful, and kept working while his younger brother spent half of his inheritance on reckless living. When the younger brother finally comes home (spoiler alert) and the father receives him back, the older brother is furious. He thinks to himself, "How can our father respond with grace after everything my younger brother has done?".

Read Luke 15:25-32.

How did the older brother respond to the celebration when his younger brother came home (v. 28)?

When the older brother compared himself to his younger brother, what did he miss about himself?

When the older brother says this, what is he doing? He's comparing his sin to the younger brother. And after he does the math, he thinks he deserves grace but believes grace should be withheld from his younger brother. The Bible has a name for that attitude, it's called self-righteousness. And the crazy thing is that thinking too little of your sin can keep you from experiencing the fullness of the love of God in the same way that thinking too much of it can. So regardless, if you think you've sinned too much to come back to God—or you're more like the older brother, who doesn't really think your sin is that bad, the Bible calls us both to the same response.

The Right Response

Earlier in this study, we talked about the Beatitudes from the Sermon on the Mount. They are a list of attitudes and attributes that define a Christian. Here, Jesus outlines a proper response to sin. Jesus says:

> *Blessed are those who mourn, for they shall be comforted.*
> MATTHEW 5:4

How would you define the word "mourn?"

Think about the people you know and how they respond to sin. Would you say that most people you know mourn their sin? Why or why not?

The word "mourn" here is key, because it's a word used specifically in regards to mourning or grieving over our sin. Jesus is showing us that there is blessing, and a comfort that can only be found when we mourn over our sin. In the original language of the New Testament, the word Jesus uses for mourn goes beyond a common understanding of mourning. Mourn in Matthew 5:4 means the deepest and most heartfelt mourning a human can experience. It's a word that was most often used to describe the feelings associated with the loss of a loved one.

Many of us have taken the grace of God so for granted that we've come to the place where sin is something that troubles us, but we don't mourn over it. We live in a Christian culture that loves to immediately jump from sin to forgiveness, but in doing so we miss the critical step of mourning.

> **Think about the definition of mourning on the previous page. How closely does your view of sin line up with Jesus'? Does your sin bother you—or does your sin cause you to mourn?**

> **What sins do you feel comfortable committing and moving on from without giving them a second thought?**

No sin is small or excusable. All sin needs to be taken seriously. When you lust after a person in your heart. When you enter into a sexual relationship with someone who is not your spouse. When you respond with ungodly anger. When you allow racism to fester. When you won't forgive. When you fall into drunkenness and debauchery. When you pursue power and privilege for personal gain. When you cheat. When you lie. Fill in the blank—when you sin, the only way to truly mourn that sin is to look to the cross.

When you look to the cross you'll see Jesus there. The only man who never sinned. And you'll see Him stripped naked, tortured, and beaten within an inch of His life. You'll see nails that were driven through His hands and feet and a crown of thorns crushed into His brow. When you look to the cross, it will hit you that it was your sin that put Him there. It will hit you that Jesus Christ went through all of that because of you. And only then will you mourn.

Read 2 Corinthians 7:10. What does Scripture say is the result of truly grieving our sins?

When God sees you sincerely mourning over your sin, He will come to you, wrap His arms around you, and bless you with a comfort that can only be found in Him. According to Paul in the verse above, godly sorrow over sin leads to repentance. The word repentance means to do a 180 degree turn. It's not a one time apology, but rather, a choice to live differently. When we do this, Jesus says we will be happy. And not just your everyday run-of-the-mill kind of happy, but Jesus claims that we will experience the highest form of happiness available to us on this planet.

What would it look like to make time in your schedule to ask Jesus to reveal to you hidden sin and mourn it.

End your time together praying to God through the words of David—a man who knew how to mourn his sin—as a guide.

Search me, O God, and know my heart;
Try me and know my anxious thoughts;
And see if there be any 1ahurtful way in me,
And lead me in the everlasting way.
PSALM 139:23-24

Reading Plan

Ephesians 1:1-10

Realize the magnitude of what God has accomplished on your behalf through the cross of Christ. Forgiveness and redemption are yours.

Read Read the passage slowly and carefully with an open heart, asking the Holy Spirit to give you words of encouragement, direction, and correction.

Examine Pick a few verses and look at them more closely to gain a deeper understanding of what the Bible is saying.

Apply Consider how you will live differently in light of what you read.

Pray Pray through the passage and your application, asking God to change your heart and to change your life, based on the time you've spent in God's Word.

Reading Plan

Isaiah 61:1-4

Jesus quoted this verse at the beginning of His ministry. He came to give comfort to those who mourn their sin.

Read Read the passage slowly and carefully with an open heart, asking the Holy Spirit to give you words of encouragement, direction, and correction.

Examine Pick a few verses and look at them more closely to gain a deeper understanding of what the Bible is saying.

Apply Consider how you will live differently in light of what you read.

Pray Pray through the passage and your application, asking God to change your heart and to change your life, based on the time you've spent in God's Word.

Reading Plan

Psalm 139:1-24

In order to realize where we have sin lurking in our hearts, it is imperative we ask God to search us and reveal to us hidden patterns of sin.

Read   Read the passage slowly and carefully with an open heart, asking the Holy Spirit to give you words of encouragement, direction, and correction.

Examine   Pick a few verses and look at them more closely to gain a deeper understanding of what the Bible is saying.

Apply   Consider how you will live differently in light of what you read.

Pray   Pray through the passage and your application, asking God to change your heart and to change your life, based on the time you've spent in God's Word.

Reading Plan

Mark 14:3-9

Realizing the grace we have received from Jesus brings a profound response like the one we see here in Mark's gospel.

Read   Read the passage slowly and carefully with an open heart, asking the Holy Spirit to give you words of encouragement, direction, and correction.

Examine   Pick a few verses and look at them more closely to gain a deeper understanding of what the Bible is saying.

Apply   Consider how you will live differently in light of what you read.

Pray   Pray through the passage and your application, asking God to change your heart and to change your life, based on the time you've spent in God's Word.

Week 8

The Reunion

Start

Last week you were challenged to mourn your sin. How is this approach to sin radically different than the way our culture typically responds to sin?

We've made it. The young man has finally completed his journey. He's rounding the last bend to the house, and he can see it now in the distance. The house, the front porch. The livestock grazing in the pastures that leads to his father's home. The familiarity of the scene no doubt gave him a sense of relief mixed with the wild uncertainty of what might unfold in the next few minutes. He looks again at his home growing closer by the second, and then he sees something he could've never expected. Still in the distance, waiting on the front porch, is his father.

Share about a time when you received grace that you didn't deserve.

Ask someone to read Luke 15:20-24.

Pray and ask God to use our time together.
After praying, watch the video teaching.

Watch

Use this section to take notes as you watch video session 8.

Video sessions available at lifeway.com/ProdigalSon
or with a subscription to smallgroup.com

Discuss

After viewing the video, discuss the following questions with your group.

As the young man rounds the corner on the last stretch of his long walk home, he must have been wondering how his father would receive him. Would he be stern? Enraged? Disappointed? Dismissive? Jesus subverts our expectations as the story concludes.

> What is surprising about the father's reaction? How would you expect a father to act in this situation?

> Jesus seems to suggest the father saw the son in the distance because he was looking for him. What does this teach us about God?

Despite the ways his son had wounded him, he never stopped looking, straining his eyes toward the distance, hoping against hope that one day he would look up and see his son walking over the horizon. What Jesus is teaching us in this story is that we have a heavenly Father who never gives up on His kids.

> Jesus teaches that God never gives up on us. If that's true, why are we so willing to believe He has?

> Why is it important for us to realize that when we return to God we are celebrated, not shamed?

> Matt ended his video teaching with an important question, do you believe the best life is found at home with your heavenly Father? If so, how has the prodigal son helped solidify that truth in your heart? If not, what doubts remain?

> What is your most important takeaway from our time in the prodigal son?

Close your discussion with prayer. Remind those in your group to complete the personal studies and Bible reading over the next week.

Personal Study 1

The God Who Won't Turn Away

Have you ever been tempted to think that you've messed up so badly or so frequently that God will throw His hands up and say "enough!"? If so, when?

Reading the story of the prodigal son, it's natural to wonder what the young man was thinking on that long walk home. Jesus describes his thoughts in the pigpen and we see him mourn his sin and prepare a speech that he hopes will earn a place back in this father's house as a servant. Then we see him stand up and begin the journey.

From that moment, Jesus jumps to describe the reunion. But Jesus doesn't recount what must've been a nerve-wracking trip. No doubt, the prodigal spent a lot of time rehearsing his speech. He likely spent a good portion of the journey beating himself up—wondering how he got into this situation in the first place. It's reasonable to speculate that as he made the trek home he wondered how his dad would respond—and he was probably preparing for a worst-case scenario.

While Jesus never explicitly says what the prodigal was thinking, from personal experience, it's safe to say the young man was anxious, and rightfully so. We all have stories of authority figures in our lives responding in anger, even when we didn't deserve it. So you can imagine what was going through the prodigal's mind on his return home.

But what this wayward young man will soon discover, is that every second of that long journey home he spent in fear and self-loathing were completely unfounded—for what was waiting for him was not a father who had written him off. But rather, a father who loved him with a love so fierce and a grace so unending that it was beyond his ability to comprehend. Today we're going to look at the God who loves us this way

God is For Us.

Read Romans 8:31-39.

If you are "for" someone or something, what does that entail? What does it mean for God to be "for"us?

When are you most tempted to believe that God isn't for you?

According to verses 32-34, what has God done to show that He is for us?

Like the prodigal's father, God is not waiting for us on the front porch, arms crossed, ready to rebuke us. At every moment of your life, God is for you. When you are walking with Him or walking away from Him, God is for you. How can we know this? Paul says that God cares so much about you that He gave His own Son to free you from being bound to sin. The resurrection of Jesus Christ is proof that God's love for you is limitless. Because of Jesus, nothing will ever separate us from the love of God.

Nothing Can Separate Us

In verse 35, Paul asks a series of rhetorical questions. What is the answer to all of these questions?

Look at verse 38-39. Write out a list of the things that Paul claims are unable to separate us from the love of God in Jesus.

Of the things listed in Romans 8:35,38-39 that cannot separate believers from the love of Christ, which stands out to you the most, and why?

Paul often used rhetorical question to convey a point. In this closing section of chapter 8, Paul asked one of the most important questions a person can ask: "Can anything separate me from the love of God?" (v. 35). Paul composes a list of threats we may perceive as separating us from God, arguing that none of these barriers could ever remove us from Christ's love for us. Nothing in all the world—no sin, however flagrant—could ever separate you from Jesus. Every time we return to our Father, He will run to us, embrace us, and give us the best He has to offer (Lk. 15:22-23).

If none of these things can separate us from Jesus, why do we easily believe the lie that we can somehow out sin God's love for us?

What evidence of God's love do you see in your daily life?

We live in a world where other people's love for us, most certainly has limits. As humans, we have breaking points. We have imaginary lines drawn in the sand that if someone we're in a relationship with crosses, our love can diminish or even disappear. Some of you might have even experienced that horrible reality with a parent, a friend, or even a spouse, and so it's hard not to project that fear onto God when we have crossed a serious line. But Jesus is teaching us in this parable that God doesn't work that way. He's not like us. When it comes to His kids, there's no line we can cross where He says "enough". It's never going to happen. Are there consequences for our sin? Yes, absolutely. But the consequences of sin will never include a heavenly Father who says, "I'm done loving you".

The Apostle Paul, under the guidance of God's own Spirit, wrote that nothing in all of creation will ever separate us from God's love in Christ Jesus. Brother and sister in Christ, can you hear that today—and not just hear it but believe it? God can no more stop loving you than He can stop being God. So while we are on our ridiculous trips to the faraway land, He doesn't turn around and walk away in disgust—it's actually the just opposite. Jesus is showing us in this story, that at the moment of our rebellion, He turns His eyes to the horizon and won't stop watching and waiting for you until He sees your face.

What steps can you take to be more aware of all the positive actions Christ Jesus has done/is doing for you?

End today by thanking God for the love He has shown you in Jesus. Receive His love, grace, and forgiveness anew.

Personal Study 2

The Searching God

We've spent the last eight weeks working through the story of the prodigal son, but the prodigal son is one of three parables in Luke 15. These stories were delivered in one address and each feature a lost object that is found and celebrated. Together they form one unified point; God's heart rejoices when a lost son or daughter comes back into relationship with Him. For our last personal study, let's take a look at these stories.

The God Who Finds

Read Luke 15:3-7.

How did the shepherd search for the sheep? What did he do when he found it?

The shepherd in this parable represents God. He finds that one percent of his flock had gone missing, and he doesn't write off the loss. Instead, he drops what he's doing and pours his energy into finding the lost sheep. Once he finds the sheep, he brings the sheep in close, and throws a party. The search and the celebration far exceed the perceived value of the lost sheep. Likewise, God rejoices when His lost sons and daughters are returned to His fold.

After the shepherd found the sheep, he took him back in. How can we welcome former prodigals back into the community of the church?

Next Jesus tells the story of a woman looking for a lost coin.

The God Who Looks

Read Luke 15:8-10.

How is this parable similar to and different from the parable of the lost sheep?

What does the extensive search for such a seemingly replaceable object teach us about God's care for those who are lost or wandering?

What is your attitude when someone comes back into a right relationship with God? How does it align with or differ from God's?

When the woman discovers a modest sum of money has gone missing, she looks in every nook and cranny of her home to recover the lost money. When she finds it, like the shepherd, she rejoices. She calls her neighbors together and invites them to find the same joy in her coin recovery as she did.

This parable, the like lost sheep, and the prodigal son we've been studying for the last eight sessions, give us a glimpse inside the heart of God. He is not content to sit and wait while one of His children is lost. He is the Shepherd who leaves the ninety-nine to search for the one. He is the woman who scours her house to find one coin. And He's the father who is sitting with his eyes fixed on the horizon.

The God Who Runs

So he got up and came to his father. But while he was still
a long way off, his father saw him and felt compassion for
him, and ran and embraced him and kissed him.

LUKE 15:20

With these words, Jesus shows us that all our fears about a God waiting to punish, shame, or rebuke us because of our sin is simply wrong. When the father looked at the horizon, maybe for the thousandth time, and finally saw his son walking home, he responds in a way that ought to bring tears to the eyes of sinners like us. When the father sees his son finally returning, his very first response was not to think to himself, "Well, there he is. The loser has come home." He doesn't yell in the house, "Hey, do you all remember my son? Yeah, the one squandered my money. He's back. Let's see how this turns out." No. Those responses are how sinful people respond to other sinful people.

Jesus tells us that when the father finally saw the son, he hiked up his robe around his waist and took off in a dead sprint towards his son. Can you stop and imagine that for a second? The dad was probably old by this point. It had probably been years since he last ran. But that's exactly what happened when the father saw the son. It was an uncontrollable response. He threw age, dignity, and caution to the wind and sprinted toward his son.

What does the running father reveal about the heart of God?

This parables teaches us how God feels about us. Our separation from Him hurts Him more than our sin. Does our sin hurt the heart of God? Yes, of course it does. But what Jesus is trying to teach us through this picture of a running God is that there is something He longs for more than anything else. He wants you to be near to Him. He wants you home where you belong. And when you finally return, there's a joy that fills His heart that overwhelms anything you might have done.

The son has come home. The father ran to him, embraced him, and clothed him with a robe and a ring. He ordered his servants to kill a fattened-calf and prepare for the party of the year. But before the party begins, the father says one more thing:

> *For this son of mine was dead and has come to life again; he*
> *was lost and has been found.' And they began to celebrate.*
> LUKE 15:24

With those final words of the father, Jesus is teaching us one final lesson. It's a benediction of sorts that sums up and ties a bow on everything He hoped we'd learn from the story of the Prodigal Son. In a way, this is Jesus' thesis sentence—one sentence that encapsulates the grand lesson of the entire parable. The father says, "My son was dead, now he is alive". With those words, Jesus is making a bold and final claim. The faraway land of sin = death. At home with the Father = Life.

What in this study has challenged you? What has encouraged you?

Who do you know who needs to encounter the God who runs to us? When will you go to them and tell them about the God that is running after them?

End your time in this study praying that God would use your time studying the prodigal son to reassure you of His love for you.

Reading Plan
Luke 15:11-32

Stories like the prodigal son merit return visits. Read this story one last time and see what you notice that you hadn't noticed before.

Read   Read the passage slowly and carefully with an open heart, asking the Holy Spirit to give you words of encouragement, direction, and correction.

Examine   Pick a few verses and look at them more closely to gain a deeper understanding of what the Bible is saying.

Apply   Consider how you will live differently in light of what you read.

Pray   Pray through the passage and your application, asking God to change your heart and to change your life, based on the time you've spent in God's Word.

Reading Plan
Luke 17:1-4

Knowing Jesus should lead us to enthusiastically embrace and restore those who seek forgiveness.

Read — Read the passage slowly and carefully with an open heart, asking the Holy Spirit to give you words of encouragement, direction, and correction.

Examine — Pick a few verses and look at them more closely to gain a deeper understanding of what the Bible is saying.

Apply — Consider how you will live differently in light of what you read.

Pray — Pray through the passage and your application, asking God to change your heart and to change your life, based on the time you've spent in God's Word.

Reading Plan

Romans 12:1-21

The father in the prodigal acts in a countercultural way. As followers of Jesus, we embrace this countercultural love and grace as a lifestyle.

Read   Read the passage slowly and carefully with an open heart, asking the Holy Spirit to give you words of encouragement, direction, and correction.

Examine   Pick a few verses and look at them more closely to gain a deeper understanding of what the Bible is saying.

Apply   Consider how you will live differently in light of what you read.

Pray   Pray through the passage and your application, asking God to change your heart and to change your life, based on the time you've spent in God's Word.

Reading Plan
2 Corinthians 5:18-21

Our Father calls us to go into all the world and tell all who will listen how to find the reconciliation we've found as members of His family.

Read   Read the passage slowly and carefully with an open heart, asking the Holy Spirit to give you words of encouragement, direction, and correction.

Examine   Pick a few verses and look at them more closely to gain a deeper understanding of what the Bible is saying.

Apply   Consider how you will live differently in light of what you read.

Pray   Pray through the passage and your application, asking God to change your heart and to change your life, based on the time you've spent in God's Word.

How to Use This Leader Guide

Prepare to Lead

Before each session, go over the video teaching and read through the group discussion to prepare for the group meeting.

Familiarize yourself with the questions and begin thinking about how to best utilize these questions for the group you are leading. The following sections on the leader guide are given to help you facilitate the group well.

Main Point

This section summarizes the big idea of each session. Use this section to help focus your preparation and leadership during the group session.

Key Scriptures

Key passages of Scripture are listed for quick reference.

Considerations

The purpose of leading a group is to bring God's Word to the people in the group. This section is designed to help you consider and wrestle with the ideas in each session and to suggest ways to apply those truths to your group.

Pray

Use the prayer provided to close the group session.

Session 1
The Problem

Main Point

This first session introduces us to the parable of the prodigal son and the crucial question at the center of the study. More than ever before, people are asking the question, "If I go all-in with living out my Christian faith, am I missing out on the best that life has to offer?" The prodigal asked it and many of the people around us are asking the same question today.

Key Scriptures

Luke 15:11-24
Matthew 13:44

Considerations

Though this story may be familiar to many, there may be others in your group who have never heard the parable of the prodigal son. Matt goes over the story in the video teaching, but be sure to have someone read the Scripture slowly and clearly to get everyone on the same page at the beginning.

Also, be mindful that there may be people in your group asking the same question the prodigal asked. Be aware and prayerful that God will answer their questions through this study.

Pray

Ask God to give the grace to hear Him clearly through this story Jesus told. Pray for increased wisdom and understanding. Confess your belief in the Bible as God's inspired Word. Ask the Spirit to use the Scriptures and our time together to to teach, rebuke, and correct us over these next eight weeks.

Session 2

The Lie

Main Point

This session builds upon the last session and focuses on the lie that led the prodigal to wander from home—the false belief that true life is found in the far off country. If life with God is so good and satisfying, why in the world are we tempted to leave Him for what we think are greener pastures? Matt gives two answers:

1. Our sinful flesh

2. The lies of the devil

Key Scriptures

Luke 15:11-12
John 8:44

Considerations

All bad thoughts and actions are rooted in false beliefs. This section asks us to consider our beliefs in light of the choices we make. There are likely individuals in your group who have never thought about their actions this way. This session should lead us to ask what lies of the devil have we believed that are keeping us from God's best for our life.

Pray

Praise the Lord Jesus Christ that His power has overwhelmed the devil, hell, and the grave. Ask the Spirit to guide us into truth and to resist the lies of the devil. Pray that the Spirit will give us the armor of God and provide us with discernment and understanding to see the lies of the devil and trust God.

Session 3
The Step

Main Point
Jesus told the story of prodigal son so we could see his mistakes and avoid making similar ones ourselves. All sin begins with a first step. Sin is sin before it becomes temptation. The key to this session is understanding the difference between temptation and sin and knowing how to cut temptation off before it becomes sin because sin never ends well.

Key Scriptures
2 Samuel 11:1-14 (Chapters 11-12 for broader context)
James 1:14-15

Considerations
You'll want to be aware that some in your group might be considering taking a step into sin. If so, they may be raw or sensitive about the content from this session. No matter where we people are in their walk with God, we want to point out the negative consequences of sin in light of the glory of God.

Pray
Ask God that by His Spirit's power, we will be people who flee from sin and run back to Him. For those of us considering sin at this moment, ask that they will see the escape from temptation that God has provided and have the courage to take it. Give thanks to God for delivering us

Session 4
The Consequences

Main Point

In this session, we see the prodigal feel the weight of his sin. Instead of feasting at his father's table, he hungers for the pods the pigs are eating. The part of the parable clarifies a crucial truth—sin always has consequences.

Key Scriptures

Luke 15:13-16
Ecclesiastes 3:11

Considerations

Lots of folks, even Christian folks, think of sin as something that's "not a big deal." We want to help lead them to a more biblical view of sin and its consequences. The point of this session is to help them see that sin is both a big deal and that there is a better way.

If they are feeling empty, point them back to God. That emptiness they feel is God asking them to wake up. Sin never satisfies, God always does.

Pray

Thank God for placing eternity in our hearts in order that we make seek and find Him. Thank the Spirit even for allowing us to feel the consequences and weight of our sin. If there are people in this room feeling consequences, pray that they will find their comfort in Jesus and receive His forgiveness.

Session 5

The Realization

Main Point

Sin, for the believer, is a monumental waste of time. God cares so much about His work in our lives that He will not allow us to stay in sin. He always brings us back through discipline or through the leading of the Holy Spirit.

Key Scriptures

Luke 15:17
Philippians 1:6
John 16:7-8

Considerations

Pay particular attention to the two people Matt addresses at the end of the video teaching—those considering sin and those stuck in a pattern of sin. Do your part to help people recognize this and find their way out with empathy and understanding.

Pray

Praise God that He brings conviction and discipline in our lives that we may turn back to Him. Ask Him to bring that conviction where sin is present among group members tonight. Pray that our group might be a place where people can wrestle with sin and find encouragement and comfort in their struggles against sin.

Session 6
The Speech

Main Point

This session takes us inside the speech the prodigal was preparing to deliver to his father. Through this we see two crucial truths. First, true repentance is unqualified acknowledgment of sin against God coupled with a desire to be right with God and others who have been harmed by our sin. But the second part of the speech reveals a flaw in the son's thinking— he believed he had out sinned his father's love for him. We see in this session that it is not possible for our sin to outweigh God's love for us.

Key Scriptures

Luke 15:18-19
Psalm 51:2-4

Considerations

You will want to help your group see two things. First, their sin is always first and foremost against God.

Second, you will want to help those who feel like their sin makes them irredeemable. Even for Christians, it is common to believe that we have sinned so grievously that God will no longer accept us. This is simply not true, but breaking the hold this lie holds over so many may require time and patience. Your role as a leader is to help people see this beautiful truth and begin to take it to heart.

Pray

Pray that we will always be repentant people. Praise God that when we seek forgiveness, He always gives it. Ask Him to restore relationships broken by sin and press into our souls the reality that we can never go so far from Him that we can't return.